The Wisdom of
THEODORE ROOSEVELT

The Wisdom of
THEODORE ROOSEVELT

Edited by Donald J. Davidson

PHILOSOPHICAL
LIBRARY

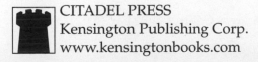
CITADEL PRESS
Kensington Publishing Corp.
www.kensingtonbooks.com

CITADEL PRESS BOOKS are published by

Kensington Publishing Corp.
850 Third Avenue
New York, NY 10022

All Kensington titles, imprints, and distributed lines are available at special quantity discounts for bulk purchases for sales promotions, premiums, fund-raising, educational, or institutional use. Special book excerpts or customized printings can also be created to fit specific needs. For details, write or phone the office of the Kensington special sales manager: Kensington Publishing Corp., 850 Third Avenue, New York, NY 10022, attn: Special Sales Department, phone 1-800-221-2647.

First Wisdom Library printing: April 2003

10 9 8 7 6 5 4 3 2 1

Printed in the United States of America

Library of Congress Control Number: 2002113397

ISBN 0-8062-2482-7

CONTENTS

PREFACE

Theodore Roosevelt, twenty-sixth president of the United States (1901–09), was born October 27, 1858, and died January 5, 1919. His sixty years spanned the period from the Civil War to the end of the First World War.

Roosevelt entered political life in 1881. From then until his death, he never ceased to be involved with politics, either as an office holder or a candidate for office, an administrator or manager, or as a national leader and irritant to Republican Party stalwarts. He was, successively, New York State assemblyman, 1882–84, candidate for New York mayor, 1886, U.S. civil-service commissioner, 1889–94, New York City police commissioner, 1895–97, assistant secretary of the navy, 1897–98, governor of New York State, 1899–1900, vice president of the United States, 1901, and then president, 1901—all of this by the age of forty-two.

Roosevelt was a complex man. To his career as politician can be added rancher, historian, naturalist, soldier, and explorer. Finally, and not least, he was a literary man, undoubtedly the best among our presidents, not excluding Jefferson, Adams, Madison, Lincoln, and Wilson. He was the author of published histories (*The Naval War of 1812*, 1882; *The Winning of the West*, 1889–96; *New York*, 1891), biographies (*Gouverneur Morris*, 1888; *Thomas Hart Benton*, 1887; *Oliver Cromwell*, 1900), papers in natural history ("Protective Coloration," 1910) and exploration (*Through the Brazilian Wilderness*, 1914) and memoirs and travel narratives (*Hunting Trips of a Ranchman*, 1885; *Ranch Life and the*

Hunting Trail, 1888; *African Game Trails*, 1910) and numerous book reviews and reflective essays. To these must be added voluminous letters, speeches, addresses, and his own marvelous memoirs, *Theodore Roosevelt: An Autobiography*, 1913. His collected works, published in 1926, ran to twenty-four volumes. Much has been added to the record since his death. Eight volumes of his correspondence have been published in *The Letters of Theodore Roosevelt*, edited by Elting M. Morison (1951–54), and there have been other collections; taken altogether they still comprise a small sample of those he wrote in his lifetime.

Roosevelt's military career was brief, but electrifying. As colonel in the Rough Riders, the volunteer cavalry unit that fought in Cuba during the Spanish-American War, he became a national hero, and fame propelled him into the governorship of New York State and then to the vice presidency.

For an American of his era, Roosevelt had an unusually deep acquaintance with the world. As a child in a wealthy family, he was educated at home, by family and tutors, and twice traveled to Europe, and once to Egypt. He graduated from Harvard University and studied law in New York City. As a young man, he was a rancher and a deputy sheriff in the Dakota Territory; he crisscrossed the United States several times in his political career; he hunted animals everywhere, including Maine and the Adirondacks, the American plains, the Mississippi Valley, the American Southwest, Africa, and South America. He associated with ranchers and hunters and farmers at one end of the social scale and with foxhunters and socialites at the other—and he was friends with all. He could sleep on the ground in the Dakotas and discuss Icelandic sagas in Washington, scale Mont Blanc and swim the Potomac, celebrate with cowboys and address a banquet. He had conquered his fears and was not afraid to descend in a submarine or fly in a rickety airplane, stand up to a lion's charge or to corporate America. He could wade in an Amazonian river or deliver a lecture to the American Historian Association, of which he was president.

He was widely known as a politician when a very young man, and the circle of his acquaintances, high and low, was vast. He was deeply liked (and disliked) and admired (and criticized). He spoke and wrote forthrightly, and he loved a good fight. He gave us as legacy the expressions "bully pulpit," "muckraker," "strenuous life," "man in the arena," and much more. In his years in the presidency he stood forthrightly for the regulation of corporations, just then developing vast economic powers, and for the preservation of our nation's natural resources.

It was his work for conservation that was perhaps his greatest contribution. During his seven-and-one-half years in the White House, Roosevelt placed almost 230 million acres under public protection as national parks, national forests, game and bird preserves, and other federal reservations (a land area equivalent to that of all the East Coast states from Maine to Florida). But he was not single-minded on the subject: his Forest Service also opened up national forests for logging, and his Reclamation Bureau built dams to provide water for farmers.

Roosevelt did not fear to use and expand the power of the presidency, as he did in the building of the Panama Canal or in opposition to European powers, nor to make a show of power by sending the American fleet around the world. His achievements in office included intervention in the anthracite coal strike of 1902, the creation of the Department of Commerce and Labor, enactment of the Elkins Act, the Hepburn Act, the Meat Inspection Act, and the Pure Food and Drug Act. He won the Nobel Peace Prize for negotiating an end to the Russo-Japanese War, and he was a lifelong advocate of a strong navy and national preparedness.

Roosevelt had a large family and reveled in family life. He was married twice. His first wife, Alice Lee, died immediately after giving birth to baby Alice. He married a second time, to Edith Carow, a childhood playmate; they had five children. He delighted in his six children, a rambunctious group, and carried on with them a correspondence both delightful and sensible, and remarkably open and adult.

As a Harvard student, he remarked that he thought he had a "second-rate brain" but a capacity for action. He was better than that. He once lamented, "What is most needed is not the ability to see what very few people can see, but to see what almost anybody can see, but nobody takes the trouble to look at." Roosevelt, as he matured, saw deeply into American society and its problems, and he sought to mobilize the people to deal with them. To us all he gave a remarkable model of the active, engaged citizen, who put his heart and soul into his work, all of it.

EDITOR'S NOTE

The Wisdom of Theodore Roosevelt has two parts. The first contains quotations taken from his speeches, articles, letters, and other writings. Quotations within sections are given in date order. Short forms are used to identify sources. If not otherwise sourced, quotations are taken from *The Works of Theodore Roosevelt* (National Edition), 20 vols. (New York: Scribner's, 1926), or from the title work as separately printed.

Short forms used in the credits:

Autobiography	*Theodore Roosevelt: An Autobiography.* New York: Macmillan, 1913.
Bishop	*Theodore Roosevelt and His Time: Shown in His Own Letters.* New York: Scribner's, 1920.
Letters	*The Letters of Theodore Roosevelt*, ed. Elting E. Morison. 8 vols. Cambridge, Mass.: Harvard University Press, 1951–54.
Wister	*Roosevelt: The Story of a Friendship.* New York: Macmillan, 1930.

The second part contains a few representative articles and speeches. They are presented entire (or, in three instances, abridged) to show not just the scope of Roosevelt's thought but also the vigor of his expression and style.

Part I

THE QUOTATIONS

America and Americans
Our nation is that one among all the nations of the earth
which holds in its hands the fate of the coming years.
"True Americanism," The Forum, April 1894

To bear the name of American is to bear the most honorable
[of] titles; and whoever does not so believe has no business
to bear the name at all, and, if he comes from Europe, the
sooner he goes back there the better.
"True Americanism," The Forum, April 1894

If of two families in a neighborhood one is perpetually gos-
siping about and criticizing the other, with a querulous,
jealous insistency in faultfinding, it is in reality the gossip-
ing family, not the other, which betrays the greater sensitiveness. The newspapers of both the United States and
England are on a common—and low—level in this respect;
but a comparison of the upper class of American and
English magazines will show that there are in the former
very few pages dealing with English morals and manners,
whether for blame or for praise, whereas the latter teem
with foolish and abusive articles about the United States.
These articles are rarely read here unless they contain some
unusually flagrant absurdity, in which case they are greed-
ily seized by the jaded editors of the press and clipped into
material for the "funny" columns. Our corresponding writ-
ers have no such morbid desire to criticise England's shortcomings. We are not interested in them. We have plenty of
problems to solve for ourselves, and it is these that interest

us; moreover, taking us as a whole, we care but little for foreign criticism of our methods of solution.

"A Colonial Survival," Cosmopolitan
Magazine, December 1892

Our country has been populated by pioneers, and therefore it has more energy, more enterprise, more expansive power than any other in the wide world.

"National Duties," speech at Minnesota State
Fair, September 2, 1901

The American people are slow to wrath, but when their wrath is once kindled it burns like a consuming flame.

First annual message to Congress,
December 3, 1901

I have a great deal of faith in the average American citizen. I think he is a pretty good fellow.

Speech at Topeka, Kansas, May 1, 1903

We are the heirs of the ages. . . .

Inaugural address, March 4, 1905

This country will not be a good place for any of us to live in if it is not a reasonably good place for all of us to live in.

"What a Progressive Is," address at Louisville,
Kentucky, April 3, 1912

In the long run this country will not be a good place for any of us to live in unless it is a reasonably good place for all of us to live in. . . .

"The Recall of Judicial Decisions," address at
Philadelphia, April 10, 1912

We believe that this country will not be a permanently good place for any of us to live in unless we make it a reasonably good place for all of us to live in.

"The Case Against the Reactionaries,"
speech at the Republican National
Convention, Chicago, June 17, 1912

"America First"

The present [Wilson] Administration, with its inveterate fondness for Ephraim's diet,* and its conviction that phrase-making is an efficient substitute for action, has plumed itself on the sentence, "America First." . . . In practice it has acted on the theory of "America Last," both at home and abroad, both in Mexico and on the high seas.

Fear God and Take Your Own Part, 1916

The American Boy

Of course what we have a right to expect of the American boy is that he shall turn out to be a good American man. Now, the chances are strong that he won't be much of a man unless he is a good deal of a boy. He must not be a coward or a weakling, a bully, a shirk, or a prig. He must work hard and play hard. He must be clean-minded and clean-lived, and able to hold his own under all circumstances and against all comers. It is only on these conditions that he will grow into the kind of American man of whom America can be really proud.

"The American Boy," St. Nicholas Magazine,
May 1900

---

* "Ephraim's diet" may refer to Isaiah 9:21, "No man spared his country-man. They snatched on the right, but remained hungry, and consumed on the left without being sated. Each devoured the flesh of his own kindred. . . ."

A healthy-minded boy should feel hearty contempt for the coward, and even more hearty indignation for the boy who bullies girls or small boys, or tortures animals.
Ibid.

Americanism

Americanism is a question of spirit, conviction, and purpose, not of creed or birthplace.
"True Americanism," The Forum, April 1894

The one absolutely certain way of bringing this nation to ruin, of preventing all possibility of its continuing to be a nation at all, would be to permit it to become a tangle of squabbling nationalities.
"Americanism," address before the Knights of Columbus,
Carnegie Hall, New York, October 12, 1915;
in Fear God and Take Your Own Part, 1916

The events of the last few years have made it evident that in this country we should not only refuse to tolerate a divided allegiance but also that we should insist on one speech. We must have in this country but one flag, the American flag, and for the speech of the people but one language, the English language.
"The Children of the Crucible," in The Foes of
Our Own Household, 1917

Americans Abroad

Every missionary, every traveler in wild lands, should know, and is inexcusable for not knowing, that the American Government has no power to pay the ransom of anyone who happens to be captured by brigands or savages. . . . If a man goes out as a missionary he has no kind of business to venture to wild lands with the expectation that somehow the Government will protect him as well as if he stayed at home. If he is fit for his work he accepts the risk as an incident to the work and has no more right to complain of what may befall him than a soldier has in getting shot. . . .

TR to Alvey August Adee, October 2, 1901,
Letters

Anarchists and Anarchism

The wind has been sowed by the men who preach such doctrines, and they cannot escape their responsibility for the whirlwind that is reaped. . . . If ever anarchy is triumphant, its triumph will last for but one red moment, to be succeeded for ages by the gloomy night of despotism.

First annual message to Congress,
December 3, 1901

Armageddon

Our cause is the cause of justice for all in the interest of all. The present contest is but a phase of the larger struggle. Assuredly the fight will go on whether we win or lose; but it will be a sore disaster to lose. What happens to me is not of the slightest consequence; I am to be used, as in a doubtful battle any man is used, to his hurt or not, so long as he is useful, and is then cast aside or left to die. I wish you to feel this. I mean it; and I shall need no sympathy when you are through with me, for this fight is far too great to permit us to concern ourselves about any one man's welfare. If we are true to ourselves by putting far above our own interests the triumph of the high cause for which we battle we shall not lose. It would be far better to fail honorably for the cause we champion than it would be to win by foul methods the foul victory for which our opponents hope. But the victory shall be ours, and it shall be won as we have already won so many victories, by clean and honest fighting for the loftiest causes. We fight in honorable fashion for the good of mankind; fearless of the future; unheeding of our individual fates; with unflinching hearts and undimmed eyes; we stand at Armageddon, and we battle for the Lord.

Peroration of "The Case Against the Reactionaries," speech at the Republican National Convention, Chicago, Illinois, June 17, 1912

Six weeks ago, here in Chicago, I spoke to the honest representatives of a convention which was not dominated by honest men; a convention wherein sat, alas! a majority of men who, with sneering indifference to every principle of right, so acted as to bring to a shameful end a party which had been founded over a half-century ago by men in whose souls burned the fire of lofty endeavor. Now to you men, who, in your turn, have come together to spend and be spent in the endless crusade against wrong, to you who face the future resolute and confident, to you who strive in a spirit of brotherhood for the betterment of our nation, to you who gird yourselves for this great new fight in the never-ending warfare for the good of humankind, I say in closing what in that speech I said in closing: We stand at Armageddon, and we battle for the Lord.

"A Confession of Faith," address before the national convention of the Progressive Party in Chicago, August 6, 1912

Army Uniforms

The first requisite in the service uniform is absolute ease and freedom. Anything that binds the body, particularly the knees, hips and arms, and anything that confines the neck, is all wrong. . . . The present shirt is all right in material, but dark blue is one of the worst possible colors for actual campaign use. The shirt should invariably be of a neutral tint, like gray or brown.

TR to William Cary Sanger, October 8, 1901, Letters

A Big Stick

I have always been fond of the West African proverb: "Speak softly and carry a big stick; you will go far." If I had not carried the big stick the organization would not have gotten behind me, and if I had yelled and blustered as Parkhurst and the similar dishonest lunatics desired, I would not have had ten votes. But I was entirely good-humored, kept perfectly cool and steadfastly refused to listen to anything save that [Lou] Payn [New York State superintendant of insurance] had to go, and that I would take none but a thoroughly upright and capable man in his place. Unless there is some cataclysm, these tactics will be crowned with success.

> *TR to Henry L. Sprague, January 26, 1900,*
> *Letters*

A good many of you are probably acquainted with the old proverb: "Speak softly and carry a big stick—you will go far." If a man continually blusters, if he lacks civility, a big stick will not save him from trouble; but neither will speaking softly avail, if back of the softness there does not lie strength, power.

> *"National Duties," speech at Minnesota*
> *State Fair, September 2, 1901*

Boasting and blustering are as objectionable among nations as among individuals, and the public men of a great nation owe it to their sense of national self-respect to speak courteously of foreign powers, just as a brave and self-respecting man treats all around him courteously. But though to boast is bad, and causelessly to insult another, worse; yet worse than all is it to be guilty of boasting, even without insult, and when called to the proof to be unable to make such boasting good. There is a homely old adage which runs: "Speak softly and carry a big stick; you will go far." If the

American Nation will speak softly, and yet build, and keep at a pitch of the highest training, a thoroughly efficient navy, the Monroe Doctrine will go far.
> *"The Monroe Doctrine," speech at Chicago, Illinois, April 2, 1903*

Books

I find reading a great comfort. People often say to me that they do not see how I find time for it, to which I answer them (much more truthfully than they believe) that to me it is a dissipation, which I have sometimes to try to avoid, instead of an irksome duty.
> *TR to George Otto Trevelyan, May 28, 1904, Letters*

Personally the books by which I have profited infinitely more than by any others have been those in which profit was a by-product of the pleasure; that is, I read them because I enjoyed them, because I liked reading them, and the profit came in as part of the enjoyment.
> *Autobiography, 1913*

Books are all very well in their way, and we love them at Sagamore Hill; but children are better than books. . . .
> *Ibid.*

Bull Moose

I wish in this campaign to do whatever you think wise and advisable—whatever is likely to produce the best results for the republican ticket. I am as strong as a bull moose and you can use me to the limit. . . .
> *TR to Mark Hanna, June 17, 1900, Letters*

Friends, I shall ask you to be as quiet as possible. I don't know whether you fully understand that I have just been shot; but it takes more than that to kill a Bull Moose.

"The Leader and the Cause," address at
Milwaukee, Wisconsin, October 14, 1912

A Bully Pulpit

I suppose my critics will call that preaching, but I have got such a bully pulpit!

Quoted in Lyman Abbott, "A Review of
President Roosevelt's Administration,"
The Outlook, February 27, 1909

Campaign Contributions

I again recommend a law prohibiting all corporations from contributing to the campaign expenses of any party. Such a bill has already passed one House of Congress. Let individuals contribute as they desire; but let us prohibit in effective fashion all corporations from making contributions for any political purpose, directly or indirectly.

Sixth annual message to Congress,
December 3, 1906

Character

And character is far more important than intellect in making a man a good citizen or successful at his calling—meaning by character not only such qualities as honesty and truthfulness, but courage, perseverance and self-reliance.

" 'Professionalism' in Sports," North
American Review, August 1890

It is always better to be an original than an imitation, even when the imitation is of something better than the original; but what shall we say of the fool who is content to be an imitation of something worse?

"True Americanism," The Forum, April 1894

Reading through the pages of history you come upon nation after nation in which there has been a high average of individual strength, bravery, and hardihood, and yet in which there has been nothing approaching to national greatness, because those qualities were not supplemented by others just as necessary. With the courage, with the hardihood, with the strength, must come the power of self-restraint, the power of self-mastery, the capacity to work for and with others as well as for one's self, the power of giving to others the love which each of us must bear for his neighbor, if we are to make our civilization really great.

Speech at Topeka, Kansas, May 1, 1903

It is character that counts in a nation as in a man. It is a good thing to have a keen, fine intellectual development in a nation, to produce orators, artists, successful businessmen; but it is an infinitely greater thing to have those solid qualities which we group together under the name of character—sobriety, steadfastness, the sense of obligation toward one's neighbor and one's God, hard common sense, and, combined with it, the lift of generous enthusiasm toward whatever is right. These are the qualities which go to make up true national greatness.

"Grant," speech at Galena, Illinois,
April 27, 1900

A man may neglect his political duties because he is too lazy, too selfish, too short-sighted, or too timid; but whatever the reason may be it is certainly an unworthy reason, and it shows either a weakness or worse than a weakness in the man's character.

"Athletics, Scholarship, and Public Service,"
address to Harvard Union, Cambridge,
Massachusetts, February 23, 1907

Let the watchwords of all our people be the old familiar watchwords of honesty, decency, fair-dealing, and common sense.

"National Unity versus Class Cleavage,"
Labor Day address at New York State Fair,
Syracuse, New York, September 7, 1903

From the greatest to the smallest, happiness and usefulness are largely found in the same soul, and the joy of life is won in its deepest and truest sense only by those who have not shirked life's burdens.

Ibid.

The same qualities that make a decent boy make a decent man. They have different manifestations, but fundamentally they are the same. If a boy has not got pluck and honesty and common sense he is a pretty poor creature; and he is a worse creature if he is a man and lacks any one of those three traits.

"The Journey on the Ridge Crest," speech at
the Prize-Day Exercises at Groton School,
May 24, 1904

In the last analysis, the most important elements in any man's career must be the sum of those qualities which, in the aggregate, we speak of as character. If he has not got it, then no law that the wit of man can devise, no administration of the law by the boldest and strongest executive, will avail to help him. We must have the right kind of character—character that makes a man, first of all, a good man in the home, a good father, a good husband—that makes a man a good neighbor.

"The New Nationalism," speech at Osawatomie,
Kansas, August 31, 1910

A man can of course hold public office, and many a man does hold public office, and lead a public career of a sort, even if there are other men who possess secrets about him which he cannot afford to have divulged. But no man can lead a public career really worth leading, no man can act with rugged independence in serious crises, nor strike at great abuses, nor afford to make powerful and unscrupulous foes, if he is himself vulnerable in his private character.

> *Autobiography, 1913*

If a man does not have an ideal and try to live up to it, then he becomes a mean, base and sordid creature, no matter how successful. If, on the other hand, he does not work practically, with the knowledge that he is in the world of actual men and must get results, he becomes a worthless head-in-the-air creature, a nuisance to himself and to everybody else.

> *TR to Kermit Roosevelt, January 27, 1915,*
> *Letters*

Character Assassination

An epidemic of indiscriminate assault upon character does not good, but very great harm. The soul of every scoundrel is gladdened whenever an honest man is assailed, or even when a scoundrel is untruthfully assailed.

> *"The Man with the Muck-Rake," address*
> *at the laying of the cornerstone of the*
> *office building of the House of Representatives,*
> *Washington, D.C., April 14, 1906*

The effort to make financial or political profit out of the destruction of character can only result in public calamity. Gross and reckless assaults on character, whether on the stump or in newspaper, magazine, or book, create a morbid and vicious public sentiment, and at the same time act as a

profound deterrent to able men of normal sensitiveness and tend to prevent them from entering the public service at any price.
Ibid.

Checks and Balances

It is often said that ours is a government of checks and balances. But this should only mean that these checks and balances obtain as among the several different kinds of representatives of the people—judicial, executive, and legislative—to whom the people have delegated certain portions of their power. It does not mean that the people have parted with their power or cannot resume it. The "division of powers" is merely the division among the representatives of the powers delegated to them; the term must not be held to mean that the people have divided their power with their delegates. The power is the people's, and only the people's.

"A Charter of Democracy," address before
the Ohio Constitutional Convention at
Columbus, Ohio, February 21, 1912

Childhood and Children

It is no use to preach to [children] if you do not act decently yourself.

Speech to Holy Name Society, Oyster Bay,
New York, August 16, 1903

But for unflagging interest and enjoyment, a household of children, if things go reasonably well, certainly makes all other forms of success and achievement lose their importance by comparison.

Autobiography, 1913

Citizenship

The first requisite of a good citizen in this Republic of ours is that he shall be able and willing to pull his weight. . . .

Address to the Chamber of Commerce of
the State of New York, New York City,
November 11, 1902

Measure iniquity by the heart, whether a man's purse be full or empty, partly full or partly empty. If the man is a decent man, whether well off or not well off, stand by him; if he is not a decent man stand against him, whether he be rich or poor. Stand against him in no spirit of vengeance, but only with the resolute purpose to make him act as decent citizens must act if this Republic is to be, and to be kept, what it shall become.

"With Malice Toward None," speech at
Oyster Bay, July 4, 1906

There is little use for the being whose tepid soul knows nothing of the great and generous emotion, of the high pride, the stern belief, the lofty enthusiasm, of the men who quell the storm and ride the thunder.

"Citizenship in a Republic," speech at
the Sorbonne, Paris, April 23, 1910

Collective Bargaining

I believe this practice of collective bargaining, effective only through such organizations as the trade unions, to have been one of the most potent forces in the past century in promoting progress of wage earners and in securing larger social progress for humanity. Wherever there is organized capital on a considerable scale I believe in the principle of organized labor and in the practice of collective bargaining, not merely as a desirable thing for the wage earners, but as something which has been demonstrated to be essential in the long run to their permanent progress. Where capital is organized, as it must be organized under modern industrial conditions, the only way to secure proper freedom—proper treatment—for the individual laborer is to have labor organize also.

"Labor and Capital," speech at Fargo,
North Dakota, September 5, 1910

Congress

There are several eminent statesmen at the other end of Pennsylvania Avenue whom I would gladly lend to the Russian Government, if they cared to expend them as bodyguards for grand dukes whenever there was a likelihood of dynamite being exploded!

TR to Cecil Arthur Spring Rice,
February 27, 1905, Letters

Congress does from a third to a half of what I think is the minimum that it ought to do, and I am profoundly grateful that I get as much.

TR to Leonard Wood, March 9, 1905, Letters

Conservation

More and more, as it becomes necessary to preserve the game, let us hope that the camera will largely supplant the rifle.

Preface to Camera Shots at Big Game,
by A. G. Wallihan, 1901

We have a right to expect that the best trained, the best educated men on the Pacific slope, the Rocky Mountains, and great plains States will take the lead in the preservation and right use of the forests, in securing the right use of the waters, and in seeing to it that our land policy is not twisted from its original purpose, but is perpetuated by amendment, by change when such change is necessary in the life of that purpose, the purpose being to turn the public domain into farms each to be the property of the man who actually tills it and makes his home on it.

Address at Leland Stanford, Junior, University,
Palo Alto, California, May 12, 1903

We of an older generation can get along with what we have, though with growing hardship; but in your full manhood and womanhood you will want what nature once so bountifully supplied and man so thoughtlessly destroyed; and because of that want you will reproach us, not for what we have used, but for what we have wasted. . . . So any nation which in its youth lives only for the day, reaps without sowing, and consumes without husbanding, must expect the penalty of the prodigal whose labor could with difficulty find him the bare means of life.

"Arbor Day: A Message to the School-Children
of the United States," April 15, 1907

Optimism is a good characteristic, but if carried to an excess it becomes foolishness. We are prone to speak of the resources of this country as inexhaustible; this is not so.

Seventh annual message to Congress,
December 3, 1907

Conservation means development as much as it does protection. I recognize the right and duty of this generation to develop and use the natural resources of our land; but I do not recognize the right to waste them, or to rob, by wasteful use, the generations that come after us.

"The New Nationalism," speech at Osawatomie,
Kansas, August 31, 1910

That farmer is a poor creature who skins the land and leaves it worthless to his children. The farmer is a good farmer who, having enabled the land to support himself and to

provide for the education of his children, leaves it to them a little better than he found it himself.
Ibid.

There can be no greater issue than that of conservation in this country.
*"A Confession of Faith," speech at the
national convention of the Progressive Party,
Chicago, Illinois, August 6, 1912*

The United States at this moment occupies a lamentable position as being perhaps the chief offender among civilized nations in permitting the destruction and pollution of nature. Our whole modern civilization is at fault in the matter. But we in America are probably most at fault. . . . We treasure pictures and sculpture. We regard Attic temples and Roman triumphal arches and Gothic cathedrals as of priceless value. But we are, as a whole, still in that low state of civilization where we do not understand that it is also vandalism wantonly to destroy or to permit the destruction of what is beautiful in nature, whether it be a cliff, a forest, or a species of mammal or bird. Here in the United States we turn our rivers and streams into sewers and dumping-grounds, we pollute the air, we destroy forests, and exterminate fishes, birds, and mammals—not to speak of vulgarizing charming landscapes with hideous advertisements.
*"Our Vanishing Wild Life," The Outlook,
January 25, 1913*

Defenders of the short-sighted men who in their greed and selfishness will, if permitted, rob our country of half its charm by their reckless extermination of all useful and beautiful wild things sometimes seek to champion them by saying that "the game belongs to the people." So it does; and not merely to the people now alive, but to the unborn people. The "greatest good for the greatest number" applies to the number within the womb of time, compared to which those now alive form but an insignificant fraction. Our duty to the whole, including the unborn generations, bids us restrain an unprincipled present-day minority from wasting the heritage of these unborn generations. The movement for the conservation of wild life and the larger movement for the conservation of all our natural resources are essentially democratic in spirit, purpose, and method.

"Bird Reserves at the Mouth of the Mississippi,"
A Book-Lover's Holidays in the Open, 1916

Constitutions

There are foolish empiricists who believe that the granting of a paper constitution, prefaced by some high-sounding declaration, of itself confers the power of self-government upon a people. This is never so. Nobody "gives" a people "self-government," any more than it is possible to "give" an individual "self-help." You know the Arab proverb runs, "God helps those who help themselves." In the long run, the only permanent way by which an individual can be helped is to help himself. . . .

"Law and Order in Egypt," address before
the National University in Cairo, Egypt,
March 28, 1910

Corporations

The great corporations which we have grown to speak of rather loosely as trusts are the creatures of the State, and the State not only has the right to control them, but it is duty bound to control them wherever the need of such control is shown. There is clearly need of supervision—need to possess the power of regulation of these great corporations through the representatives of the public—wherever, as in our own country at the present time, business corporations become so very powerful alike for beneficent work and for work that is not always beneficent. It is idle to say that there is no need of such supervision. There is, and a sufficient warrant for it is to be found in any one of the admitted evils appertaining to them.

*"The Control of Corporations," address at
Providence, Rhode Island, August 23, 1902*

I believe in corporations. If a corporation is doing square work I will help it so far as I can. If it oppresses anybody; if it is acting dishonestly towards its stockholders or the public, or towards its laborers, or towards small competitors—why, when I have power I shall try to cinch it.

*TR to Ray Stannard Baker, August 27, 1904,
Letters*

For every special interest is entitled to justice, but not one is entitled to a vote in Congress, to a voice on the bench, or to representation in any public office. The Constitution guarantees protection to property, and we must make that promise good. But it does not give the right of suffrage to any corporation.

*"The New Nationalism," speech at Osawatomie,
Kansas, August 31, 1910*

There can be no effective control of corporations while their political activity remains.

Ibid.

The people of the United States have but one instrument which they can efficiently use against the colossal combinations of business—and that instrument is the government of the United States. . . .

*"Limitation of Government Power,"
address at the Coliseum, San Francisco,
September 14, 1912*

Corruption

No prosperity and no glory can save a nation that is rotten at heart.

"National Duties," Minnesota State Fair,
St. Paul, September 2, 1901

If I were asked to name the three influences which I thought were most dangerous to the perpetuity of American institutions, I should name corruption, in business and politics alike, lawless violence, and mendacity, especially when used in connection with slander.

"The Nation and the States," speech before
the Colorado Legislature, Denver, Colorado,
August 29, 1910

There are two chief sources of danger to the American people: lawless violence and corruption; lawless violence, which we most often have to face from among the people who have least of the world's goods; and corruption, which we most often have to face from among the people that have most of the world's goods.

Speech before the Hamilton Club, Chicago,
September 8, 1910

When I was President I endeavored to act so that there should be no need of raising the cry among my opponents of "Turn the rascals out," because I turned them out myself just as fast as I could get at them.

Ibid.

There is no greater duty than to war on the corrupt and unprincipled boss, and on the corrupt and unprincipled business man; and for the matter of that, the corrupt and unprincipled labor leader also, and on the corrupt and unprincipled editor, and on anyone else who is corrupt and unprincipled.

Autobiography, 1913

Cuba

Cuba is, in my judgment, entitled ultimately to settle for itself whether it shall be an independent state or an integral portion of the mightiest of republics. But until order and stable liberty are secured, we must remain in the island to insure them, and infinite tact, judgment, moderation, and courage must be shown by our military and civil representatives in keeping the island pacified, in relentlessly stamping out brigandage, in protecting all alike, and yet in showing proper recognition to the men who have fought for Cuban liberty.

*"The Strenuous Life," speech before the
Hamilton Club, Chicago, April 10, 1899*

My dear Mr. Root:

Through you I want to send my heartiest greetings to those gathered to celebrate the second anniversary of the Republic of Cuba. I wish that it were possible to be present with you in person. I rejoice in what Cuba has done and especially in the way in which for the last two years her people have shown their desire and ability to accept in a serious spirit the responsibilities that accompany freedom. Such determination is vital, for those unable or unwilling to shoulder the responsibility of using their liberty aright can never in the long run preserve liberty.

As for the United States, it must ever be a source of joy and gratification to good American citizens that they were enabled to play the part they did as regards Cuba. We freed Cuba from tyranny; we then stayed in the island until we had established civil order and laid the foundations for self-government and prosperity; we then made the island independent, and have since benefited her inhabitants by making closer the commercial relations between us. I hail what has been done in Cuba not merely for its own sake, but as showing the purpose and desire of this nation toward all the nations south of us. It is not true that the United States has any land hunger or entertains any projects as regards other nations, save such as are for their welfare.

All that we desire is to see all neighboring countries stable, orderly and prosperous. Any country whose people conduct themselves well can count upon our hearty friendliness. If a nation shows that it knows how to act with decency in industrial and political matters, if it keeps order and pays it obligations, then it need fear no interference from the United States. Brutal wrongdoing, or an impotence which results in a general loosening of the ties of civilized society, may finally require intervention by some civilized nation, and in the Western Hemisphere the United States cannot ignore this duty; but it remains true that our interests, and those of our southern neighbors, are in reality identical. All that we ask is that they shall govern themselves well, and be prosperous and orderly. Where this is the case they will find only helpfulness from us.

To-night you are gathered together to greet a young nation which has shown hitherto just those needed qualities; and I congratulate not only Cuba but also the United States upon the showing which Cuba has made.

*TR to Elihu Root, a letter read at a dinner in
New York City to celebrate Cuban independence,
May 20, 1904, Letters*

Dark Horses

The Presidential office tends to put a premium upon a man's keeping out of trouble rather than upon his accomplishing results. If a man has a very decided character, has a strongly accentuated career, it is normally the case of course that he makes ardent friends and bitter enemies; and unfortunately human nature is such that more enemies will leave their party because of enmity to its head than friends will come in from the opposite party because they think well of that same head. In consequence, the dark horse, the neutral-tinted individual, is very apt to win against the man of pronounced views and active life. The electorate is very apt to vote with its back to the future!

TR to George Otto Trevelyan, May 28, 1904,
Letters

Democracy

The welfare of each of us is dependent fundamentally upon the welfare of all of us, and therefore in public life that man is the best representative of each of us who seeks to do good to each by doing good to all; in other words, whose endeavor it is, not to represent any special class and promote merely that class's selfish interests, but to represent all true and honest men of all sections and all classes, and to work for their interests by working for our common country.

"National Unity versus Class Cleavage,"
Labor Day address at New York State Fair,
Syracuse, New York, September 7, 1903

It can not be too often repeated that in this country, in the long run, we all of us tend to go up or down together.

Ibid.

There have been many republics in the past, both in what we call antiquity and in what we call the Middle Ages. They fell, and the prime factor in their fall was the fact that the parties tended to divide along the line that separates wealth from poverty. It made no difference which side was successful; it made no difference whether the republic fell under the rule of an oligarchy or the rule of a mob. In either case, when once loyalty to a class had been substituted for loyalty to the republic, the end of the republic was at hand.

"Citizenship in a Republic," speech at
the Sorbonne, Paris, April 23, 1910

Be progressive. A great democracy must be progressive or it will soon cease to be great or a democracy. . . .
"The Nation and the States," speech before
the Colorado Legislature, Denver, Colorado,
August 29, 1910

Our country offers the most wonderful example of democratic government on a giant scale that the world has ever seen; and the peoples of the world are watching to see whether we succeed or fail. . . . We believe in all our hearts in democracy; in the capacity of the people to govern themselves; and we are bound to succeed, for our success means not only our own triumph, but the triumph of the cause of the rights of the people throughout the world, and the uplifting of the banner of hope for all the nations of mankind.
"The Republican Record and Popular Rule,"
speech at Saratoga, New York,
September 27, 1910

Constitution-makers should make it clear beyond shadow of doubt that the people in their legislative capacity have the power to enact into law any measure they deem necessary for the betterment of social and industrial conditions. The wisdom of framing any particular law of this kind is a proper subject of debate; but the power of the people to enact the law should not be subject to debate. To hold the contrary view is to be false to the cause of the people, to the cause of American democracy.
"A Charter of Democracy," address before
the Ohio Constitutional Convention at
Columbus, Ohio, February 21, 1912

We must act with justice and broad generosity and charity toward one another and toward all men if we are to make this Republic what it must and shall be made, the nation in all the earth where each man can in best and freest fashion live his own life unwronged by others and proudly careful to wrong no other man.

> *"The Heirs of Abraham Lincoln," speech*
> *at the Lincoln Day banquet, New York City,*
> *February 12, 1913*

Demagoguery

To play the demagogue for purposes of self-interest is a cardinal sin against the people in a democracy, exactly as to play the courtier for such purposes is a cardinal sin against the people under other forms of government. A man who stays long in our American political life, if he has in his soul the generous desire to do effective service for great causes, inevitably grows to regard himself merely as one of many instruments, all of which it may be necessary to use, one at one time, one at another, in achieving the triumph of those causes; and whenever the usefulness of any one has been exhausted, it is to be thrown aside. If such a man is wise, he will gladly do the thing that is next, when the time and the need come together, without asking what the future holds for him. Let the half-god play his part well and manfully, and then be content to draw aside when the god appears. Nor should he feel vain regrets that to another it is given to render greater services and reap a greater reward. Let it be enough for him that he too has served, and that by doing well he has prepared the way for the other man who can do better.

> *Autobiography, 1913*

Duty

We are a great nation and we are compelled, whether we will or not, to face the responsibilities that must be faced by all great nations. It is not in our power to avoid meeting

them. All that we can decide is whether we shall meet them
well or ill.

"America's Part of the World's Work," address
at the Lincoln Club Dinner in New York City,
February 13, 1899

If we refrain from doing our part of the world's work, it will
not alter the fact that that work has got to be done, only it
will have to be done by some stronger race, because we will
have shown ourselves weaklings.

Ibid.

If we are to be a really great people, we must strive in good
faith to play a great part in the world. We cannot avoid
meeting great issues. All that we can determine for ourselves is whether we shall meet them well or ill.

"The Strenuous Life," speech before the
Hamilton Club, Chicago, April 10, 1899

Our country shall not shirk its duty to mankind. It can perform this duty only if it is true to itself. It can be true to itself
only by definitely resolving to take the position of the just
man armed; for a proud and self-respecting nation of
freemen must scorn to do wrong to others and must also
scorn tamely to submit to wrong done by others.

Foreword to America and the World War,
1915

Efficiency

You must be efficient. You must be able to hold your own in
the world of politics, the world of business; able to keep
your head above water, to make your work satisfactory, to
make it pay. If you do not, you cannot do good to others.
You must never forget for a moment that so far from the
doctrine of efficiency being a base doctrine, it is a doctrine
vital to good in this country. If the elders as well as the boys

would keep that in mind, they would appreciate better what I regard as one of the cardinal political doctrines that should be preached ever in this country, the doctrine that we should never penalize efficiency; that the line we should draw in business is on conduct and not on size, and what we should discriminate against is misconduct in any phase, and not efficiency.

> *Address delivered at the Hill School, Pottstown, Pennsylvania, June 10, 1913*

But if a man's efficiency is not guided and regulated by a moral sense, then the more efficient he is, the more dangerous to the body politic.

> *"Citizenship in a Republic," speech at the Sorbonne, Paris, April 23, 1910*

Empire
The day when the keels of the Low Dutch seathieves first grated on the British coast was big with the doom of many nations.

> *The Winning of the West, 1889*

No sensible man will advocate our plunging rashly into a course of international knight-errantry; none will advocate our setting deliberately to work to build up a colonial empire. But neither will any brave and patriotic man bid us shrink from doing our duty merely because this duty involves the certainty of strenuous effort and the possibility of danger.

> *"America's Part of the World's Work," address at the Lincoln Club Dinner in New York City, February 13, 1899*

What the Spaniard has been taught the Malay must learn— that the American flag is to float unchallenged where it floats now. But remember this, that when this has been accomplished our task has only just begun. Where we have won entrance by the prowess of our soldiers we must deserve to continue by the righteousness, the wisdom, and the evenhanded justice of our rule. The American administrators in the Philippines, as in Cuba and Porto Rico, must be men chosen for signal capacity and integrity; men who will administer the provinces on behalf of the entire nation from which they come, and for the sake of the entire people to which they go.

Ibid.

The policy of expansion is America's historic policy. We have annexed the Philippines exactly as we have annexed Hawaii, New Mexico, and Alaska. They are now part of American territory and we have no more right to give them up than we have the right to restore Hawaii to the Kanaka Queen or to abandon Alaska to the Esquimaux.

"The Prophecies of Mr. Bryan," speech at
Detroit, Michigan, September 7, 1900

English

It seems extraordinary that it should have been left to Mr. [Brander] Matthews to formulate what so many Americans had felt—namely, that the American has precisely the same right to the English speech as the Briton. He is not the Briton's younger brother, any more than he is his elder brother. Each has an equal claim to a common inheritance— the inheritance of the great language and literature which are the most precious possessions of the two nations. If the present-day literature of either America or Great Britain depart in any way from the standards of the past—as depart it must—the departure must be judged purely on its own merits, and without the least regard to what course literature is taking in the other country at the same time. England

has no more right to set the standard for America than America has to set the standard for England.
> *"An Introduction to American Literature,"*
> *review in the Bookman, February 1896*

We should provide for every immigrant, by day-schools for the young and night-schools for the adult, the chance to learn English; and if after, say, five years he has not learned English, he should be sent back to the land from whence he came.
> *"The Children of the Crucible," in The Foes*
> *of Our Own Household, 1917; similarly in*
> *The Great Adventure, 1918*

Envy
Envy is merely the meanest form of admiration, and a man who envies another admits thereby his own inferiority.
> *Address at the University of California,*
> *Berkeley, May 14, 1903*

Envy is as evil a thing as arrogance. . . .
> *TR to Paul Estournelles de Constant,*
> *September 1, 1903, Letters*

Equality
We should not say that men are equal where they are not equal, nor proceed upon the assumption that there is an equality where it does not exist; but we should strive to bring about a measurable equality, at least to the extent of preventing the inequality which is due to force or fraud.
> *"Citizenship in a Republic," speech at the*
> *Sorbonne, Paris, April 23, 1910*

Evil

No man is justified in doing evil on the ground of expediency.

"Longitude and Latitude Among Reformers,"
The Century, January 1900

War with evil; but show no spirit of malignity toward the man who may be responsible for the evil. Put it out of his power to do wrong. . . .

"With Malice Toward None," speech at
Oyster Bay, New York, July 4, 1906

Fear

There were all kinds of things I was afraid of at first, ranging from grizzly bears to "mean" horses and gunfighters; but by acting as if I was not afraid I gradually ceased to be afraid.

Autobiography, 1913

The worst of all fears is the fear of living.

Ibid.

Germany

Of all the nations of Europe it seems to me Germany is by far the most hostile to us. With Germany under the Kaiser we may at any time have trouble if she seeks to acquire territory in South America.

TR to F. C. Moore, February 5, 1898; quoted
in Bishop, 1:79–80

Glory

It is a base untruth to say that happy is the nation that has no history. Thrice happy is the nation that has a glorious history. Far better it is to dare mighty things, to win glorious triumphs, even though checkered by failure, than to take rank with those poor spirits who neither enjoy much nor suffer much, because they live in the gray twilight that knows not victory nor defeat.

"The Strenuous Life," address before the
Hamilton Club, Chicago, April 10, 1899

Government

It behooves us to remember that men can never escape being governed. Either they must govern themselves or they must submit to being governed by others. If from lawlessness or fickleness, from folly or self-indulgence, they refuse to govern themselves, then most assuredly in the end they will have to be governed from the outside.

Speech at the opening of the Jamestown
Exposition, Virginia, April 26, 1907

The object of government is the welfare of the people. The material progress and prosperity of a nation are desirable chiefly so far as they lead to the moral and material welfare of all citizens.

"The New Nationalism," speech at Osawatomie,
Kansas, August 31, 1910

John Hay

John Hay's death was very sudden and removes from American public life a man whose position was literally unique. The country was the better because he had lived, for it was a fine thing to have set before our young men the example of success contained in the career of a man who had held so many and such important public positions, while there was not in his nature the slightest touch of the demagogue, and who in addition to his great career in political life had also left a deep mark in literature. His *Life of Lincoln* is a monument, and of its kind his *Castilian Days* is perfect.

TR to Henry Cabot Lodge, July 11, 1905,
Letters

Heroism

Every feat of heroism makes us forever indebted to the man who performed it. All daring and courage, all iron endurance of misfortune, all devotion to the idea of honor and the glory of the flag, make for a fine and nobler type of manhood. It is not only those who do and dare and endure that are benefited; but also the countless thousands who are not themselves called upon to face the peril, to show the strength, or to win the reward. All of us lift our heads higher because those of our countrymen whose trade it is to meet danger have met it well and bravely. All of us are poorer for every base or ignoble deed done by an American, for every instance of selfishness or weakness or folly on the part of the people as a whole. We are all worse off when any of us fails at any point in his duty toward the State in time of peace, or his duty toward the State in time of war. If ever we had to meet defeat at the hands of a foreign foe, or had to submit tamely to wrong or insult, every man among us worthy of the name of American would feel dishonored and debased. On the other hand, the memory of every triumph won by Americans, by just so much helps to make each American nobler and better. Every man among us is more fit to meet the duties and responsibilities of citizenship because of the perils over which, in the past, the nation has triumphed; because of the blood and sweat and tears, the labor and the anguish, through which, in the days that have gone, our forefathers moved on to triumph. There are higher things in this life than the soft and easy enjoyment of material comfort. It is through strife, or the readiness for strife, that a nation must win greatness.

"Washington's Forgotten Maxim,"
address before the Naval War College,
Newport, Rhode Island, June 2, 1897

Honesty

The eighth commandment reads: "Thou shalt not steal." It does not read: "Thou shalt not steal from the rich man." It does not read: "Thou shalt not steal from the poor man." It reads simply and plainly: "Thou shalt not steal." No good whatever will come from that warped and mock morality which denounces the misdeeds of men of wealth and forgets the misdeeds practised at their expense; which denounces bribery, but blinds itself to blackmail; which foams with rage if a corporation secures favors by improper methods, and merely leers with hideous mirth if the corporation is itself wronged. The only public servant who can be trusted honestly to protect the rights of the public against the misdeed of a corporation is that public man who will just as surely protect the corporation itself from wrongful aggression. If a public man is willing to yield to popular clamor and do wrong to the men of wealth or to rich corporations, it may be set down as certain that if the opportunity comes he will secretly and furtively do wrong to the public in the interest of a corporation.

"The Man with the Muck-Rake," address
at the laying of the cornerstone of the office
building of the House of Representatives,
Washington, D.C., April 14, 1906

Be honest, and remember that honesty counts for nothing unless back of it lie courage and efficiency.

"The Journey on the Ridge Crest," speech
at the Prize-Day Exercises at Groton School,
May 24, 1904

If a public man tries to get your vote by saying that he will do something wrong *in* your interest, you can be absolutely certain that if ever it becomes worth his while he will do something wrong *against* your interest.

"Citizenship in a Republic," speech at
the Sorbonne, Paris, April 23, 1910

Mark Twain, who was not only a great humorist, but a great philosopher, in his proverbs by Pudd'nhead Wilson, said that there are eight hundred and sixty-nine different kinds of lies, but that the only one authoritatively prohibited is bearing false witness against your neighbor. The politician—I am a politician—and the writer for periodicals or the press—and I am one again—should bear steadily in mind that the eighth and ninth commandments are equally binding: "The shalt not steal; Thou shalt not bear false witness against thy neighbor."

"The Public Press," speech at Milwaukee
Auditorium, Milwaukee, Wisconsin,
September 7, 1910

Hyphenated Americans
Above all, the one essential for success in every political movement which is to do lasting good, is that our citizens should act as Americans; not as Americans with a prefix and qualification—not as Irish-Americans, German-Americans, Native Americans—but as Americans pure and simple.

Preface to New York, 1660–1890, 1891

In any crisis the hyphenated American is an active force against America, an active force for wrongdoing. The effort to hoist two flags on the same flagpole always means that one flag is hoisted underneath, and the hyphenated American invariably hoists the flag of the United States underneath.

"This Nation's Needs," address at Plattsburgh,
New York, August 25, 1915

The hyphenated American of any type is a bad American and an enemy to this country. The best possible antiscorbutic for this danger is universal service.

Fear God and Take Your Own Part, 1916

In this war, either a man is a good American, and therefore is against Germany, and in favor of the allies of America, or he is not an American at all, and should be sent back to Germany where he belongs.

"The Children of the Crucible," in The Foes of
Our Own Household, 1917

There is no place for the hyphen in our citizenship. There is no place for a fifty-fifty Americanism in the United States. He who is not with us, absolutely and without reserve of any kind, is against us, and should be treated as an alien enemy, to be interned or sent out of the country. . . . We are a nation, not a hodge-podge of foreign nationalities. We are a people, and not a polyglot boarding house.

"The Square Deal in Americanism,"
Metropolitan, February, August 1918; in
The Great Adventure, 1918

Ideals

Be practical as well as generous in your ideals. Keep your eyes on the stars, but remember to keep your feet on the ground. Be truthful; a lie implies fear, vanity, or malevolence; be frank; furtiveness and insincerity are faults incompatible with true manliness. Be honest, and remember that honesty counts for nothing unless back of it lie courage and efficiency.

"The Journey on the Ridge Crest," speech at
the Prize-Day Exercises at Groton School,
May 24, 1904

Ignorance

Viewed from any angle, ignorance is the costliest crop that can be raised in any part of this Union.

"The Education of the Negro," address
at Tuskegee Institute, Tuskegee, Alabama,
October 24, 1905

It seems to me that you are eminently right in seeing that it is good to give a name to something of vital consequence, even tho in a sense the name only expresses our ignorance. It is a curious thing in mankind, but undoubtedly true, that if we do not give such a name to our ignorance, most of us gradually feel that there is nothing to be ignorant about.

TR to Arthur James Balfour, March 5, 1908,
Letters

Immigrants and Immigration

But in the interest of our workingmen we must in the end keep out laborers who are ignorant, vicious, and with low standards of life and comfort, just as we have shut out the Chinese.

"How Not to Help Our Poorer Brother,"
Review of Reviews, January 1897

It is urgently necessary to check and regulate our immigration, by much more drastic laws than now exist; and this should be done both to keep out laborers who tend to depress the labor market, and to keep out races which do not assimilate readily with our own, and unworthy individuals of all races—not only criminals, idiots, and paupers, but anarchists of the [Johann] Most and O'Donovan Rossa type.

"True Americanism," The Forum, April 1894

As you know, my position, announced in my message and since, has been that we want to make even more stringent the exclusion of Chinese laborers (not Chinese students or merchants). . . .

TR to Leslie Mortier Shaw, March 27, 1902, Letters

It is equally to the interest of the British Empire and of the United States that there should be no immigration in mass from Asia to Australia or to North America. It can be prevented, and an entirely friendly feeling between Japan and the English-speaking peoples preserved, if we act with sufficient courtesy and at the same time with sufficient resolution.

TR to James Arthur Balfour, March 5, 1908, Letters

We have room for but one language here, and that is the English language, for we intend to see that the crucible turns our people out as Americans, of American nationality, and not as dwellers in a polyglot boarding-house; and we have room for but one soul loyalty, and that is loyalty to the American people.

TR to the president of the American Defense Society, January 3, 1919; quoted in Bishop 2:474.

In God We Trust

When the question of the new coinage came up we lookt into the law and found there was no warrant therein for putting "IN GOD WE TRUST" on the coins. As the custom, altho without legal warrant, had grown up, however, I might have felt at liberty to keep the inscription had I approved of its being on the coinage. But as I did not approve of it, I did not direct that it should again be put on. Of course the matter of the law is absolutely in the hands of Congress, and any direction of Congress in the matter will be immediately obeyed. . . . As regards its use on the coinage we have actual experience by which to go. In all my life I have never heard any human being speak reverently of this motto on the coins or show any sign of its having appealed to any high emotion in him. But I have literally hundreds of times heard it used as an occasion of, and incitement to, the sneering ridicule which it is above all things undesirable that so beautiful and exalted a phrase should excite. . . . Everyone must remember the innumerable cartoons and articles based on phrases like "In God we trust for the other eight cents"; "In God we trust for the short weight"; "In God we trust for the thirty-seven cents we do not pay"; and so forth and so forth. Surely I am well within bounds when I say that a use of the phrase which invites constant levity of this type is most undesirable.

TR to Roland C. Dryer, November 11, 1907, Letters

Japan and the Japanese

I do not agree, however, that Japan has any immediate intention of moving against us in the Philippines. Her eyes for some time to come will be directed toward Korea and southern Manchuria. If she attacked us and met disaster, she would lose everything she has gained in the war with Russia. . . . No man can prophesy about the future, but I see not the slightest chance of Japan attacking us in the Philippines for a decade or two, or until the present conditions of international politics change.

TR to Leonard Wood, January 22, 1906, Letters

In the Japanese matter the crux is the bringing in of the Japanese laboring men. Whether we like it or not, I think we have to face the fact that the people of the Pacific slope, with the warm approval of the labor men throughout the country, will become steadily more and more hostile to the Japanese if their laborers come here, and I am doing my best to bring about an agreement with Japan by which the laborers of each country shall be kept out of the other country. . . . Personally, my view is that it does no possible good to deprive those who are here of the franchise. On the contrary I think that we should studiously give the franchise and school facilities to, and in other ways treat as well as possible, all the Japanese that come, but keep out all the laboring class.

TR to Lyman Abbott, January 3, 1907, Letters

The Judiciary

The [New York] Court of Appeals declared the law [prohibiting the manufacture of cigars in tenement houses] unconstitutional, and in their decision the judges reprobated the law as an assault upon the "hallowed" influences of "home." It was this case which first waked me to a dim and partial understanding of the fact that the courts were not necessarily the best judges of what should be done to better social and industrial conditions. The judges who rendered this decision were well-meaning men. They knew nothing whatever of tenement-house conditions; they knew nothing whatever of the needs, or the life and labor, of three-fourths of their fellow-citizens in great cities. They knew legalism, but not life. Their choice of the words "hallowed" and "home," as applicable to the revolting conditions attending the manufacture of cigars in tenement-houses, showed that they had no idea what it was that they were deciding. Imagine the "hallowed" associations of a "home" consisting of one room where two families, one of them with a boarder, live, eat, and work. This decision completely blocked tenement-house reform legislation in New York for a score of year, and hampers it to this day. It was one of the most serious setbacks which the cause of industrial and social progress and reform ever received.

I had been brought up to hold the courts in especial reverence. The people with whom I was most intimate were apt to praise the courts for just such decisions. . . . These were the same people with whom the judges who rendered these decisions were apt to foregather at social clubs, or dinners, or in private life. Very naturally they all tended to look at things from the same standpoint. Of course it took more than one experience such as this Tenement Cigar Case to shake me out of the attitude in which I was brought up. But various decisions, not only of the New York court but of certain other State courts and even of the United States Supreme Court, during the quarter of a century following the passage of this tenement-house legislation, did at last thoroughly wake me to the actual fact. I grew to realize that all that Abraham Lincoln had said about the Dred Scott decision could be said with equal truth and justice about the numerous decisions which in our own day were erected as bars across the path of social reform, and which brought to naught so much of the effort to secure justice and fair dealing for workingmen and workingwomen and for plain citizens generally.

Autobiography, 1913

Labor

The worst foe of the poor man is the labor leader, whether philanthropist or politician, who tries to teach him that he is a victim of conspiracy and injustice, when in reality he is merely working out his fate with blood and sweat as the immense majority of men who are worthy of the name always have done and always will have to do.

"How Not to Help Our Poorer Brother,"
Review of Reviews, January 1897

The welfare of the wage-worker, the welfare of the tiller of the soil, upon these depend the welfare of the entire country. . . .

"The Man with the Muck-Rake," address
at the laying of the cornerstone of the
office building of the House of Representatives,
Washington, D.C., April 14, 1906

But to attempt to leave the question of contract between employer and employee merely to individual action means the absolute destruction of individualism; for where the individual is so weak that he, perforce, has to accept whatever a strongly organized body chooses to give him, his individual liberty becomes a mere sham and mockery. It is indispensably necessary, in order to preserve to the largest degree our system of individualism, that there should be effective and organized collective action. The wage earners must act jointly, through the process of collective bargaining, in great industrial enterprises. Only thus can they be put upon a plane of economic equality with their corporate employers. Only thus is freedom of contract made a real thing and not a mere legal fiction.

"Labor and Capital," speech at Fargo,
North Dakota, September 5, 1910

No worker should be compelled, as a condition of earning his daily bread, to risk his life and limb, or be deprived of his health, or have to work under dangerous and bad surroundings. Society owes the worker this because it owes as much to itself. He should not be compelled to make this a matter of contract; he ought not to be left to fight alone for decent conditions in this respect. His protection in the place where he works should be guaranteed by the laws of the land. In other words, he should be protected during his working hours against greed and carelessness on the part of unscrupulous employers, just as outside of those working hours both he and his employer are protected in their lives and property against the murderer and the thief.

Ibid.

The old-style Bourbon capitalist was fond of insisting that the government should do nothing except keep order; that it was its highest duty by force to interfere with violence, which was the weapon of the misguided or criminal wage-worker, but that it was an abhorrent wrong for it to interfere with the greed, cunning, trickery, and ruthless indifference to the welfare of others, which were shown not only by evil capitalists, but by many well-meaning capitalists who simply did not think and did not possess foresight and vision.

> *"A Square Deal in Law Enforcement,"*
> *The Foes of Our Own Household, 1917*

At present the mass of people engaged in industry cannot become owners as individuals; and to give this mass a nominal ownership which does not imply control fails to reach the heart of the matter, for control is the element which implies equality between men. But no man is fit for control who does not possess intelligence, self-respect, and respect for the just rights of others. Therefore, instead of individual control of industry, there must today be some species of collective control of industry; which means that the tool-users shall become the tool-owners; but which also means that they will assuredly break down themselves and their business unless they are willing to pay for skilled management a price, in some measure, corresponding to the high value of the service rendered, and unless they are willing to give a just reward to whatever necessary capital they cannot themselves supply. This means an effort toward a combination of the proper functions of the corporation with the wise activities of the labor-union (and I emphasize proper in one case and wise in the other).

> *"Washington and Lincoln: The Great*
> *Examples," The Foes of Our Own*
> *Household, 1917*

Law

Ours is a government of liberty by, through, and under the law. No man is above it and no man is below it. The crime of cunning, the crime of greed, the crime of violence, are all equally crimes, and against them all alike the law must set its face.

> *"Liberty Under Law," Speech at Spokane,*
> *Washington, May 26, 1903; identically*
> *at Dallas, April 5, 1905*

While all people are foolish if they violate or rail against the law—wicked as well as foolish, but all foolish—yet the most foolish man in this Republic is the man of wealth who complains because the law is administered with impartial justice against or for him. His folly is greater than the folly of any other man who so complains; for he lives and moves and has his being because the law does in fact protect him and his property.

We have the right to ask every decent American citizen to rally to the support of the law if it is ever broken against the interest of the rich man; and we have the same right to ask that rich man cheerfully and gladly to acquiesce in the enforcement against his seeming interest of the law, if it is the law. Incidentally, whether he acquiesces or not, the law will be enforced; and this whoever he may be, great or small, and at whichever end of the social scale he may be.

> *Ibid.*

No man is above the law and no man is below it; nor do we ask any man's permission when we require him to obey it. Obedience to the law is demanded as a right; not asked as a favor.

> *Third annual message to Congress,*
> *December 7, 1903*

If people will obey the law they can count on my doing all I can to further their interests, but I will no more countenance crimes of greed and cunning by men of property than crimes of brutality and violence against property.

TR to David Scull, August 16, 1907, Letters

During the closing year and a half of my term I shall follow precisely the course I have followed during the last six years. I shall enforce the laws; I shall enforce them against men of vast wealth just exactly as I enforce them against ordinary criminals; and I shall not flinch from this course, come weal or come woe.

Ibid.

Legislators

There are plenty of decent legislators, and plenty of able legislators; but the blamelessness and the fighting edge are not always combined. Both qualities are necessary for the man who is to wage active battle against the powers that prey. He must be clean of life, so that he can laugh when his public or his private record is searched; and yet being clean of life will not avail him if he is either foolish or timid. He must walk warily and fearlessly and while he should never brawl if he can avoid it, he must be ready to hit hard if the need arises. Let him remember, by the way, that the unforgivable crime is soft hitting. Do not hit at all if it can be avoided; but *never* hit softly.

Autobiography, 1913

Life

Only those are fit to live who do not fear to die; and none are fit to die who have shrunk from the joy of life and the duty of life.

"The Great Adventure," Cosmopolitan, October 1918; in The Great Adventure, 1918

Malefactors of Great Wealth

There were continual contests for the control of railway systems, and "operations" in stocks which barely missed being criminal, and which branded those who took part in them as infamous in the sight of all honest men; and the courts and legislative bodies became parties to the iniquity of men composing that most dangerous of all classes, the wealthy criminal class.

New York, 1660–1890 (1891)

During the present trouble with the stock market I have, of course, received countless requests and suggestions, public and private, that I should say or do something to ease the situation. There is a world-wide financial disturbance. . . . Most of it I believe to be due to matters not peculiar to the United States, and most of the remainder to matters wholly unconnected with any governmental action; but it may well be that the determination of the government (in which, gentlemen, it will not waver) to punish certain malefactors of great wealth, has been responsible for something of the trouble; at least to the extent of having caused these men to combine to bring about as much financial stress as possible, in order to discredit the policy of the government and thereby secure a reversal of that policy, so that they may enjoy unmolested the fruits of their own evil-doing. That they have misled many good people into believing that there should be such reversal of policy is possible. If so I am sorry; but it will not alter my attitude. . . . There will be no change in the policy we have steadily pursued, no let up in the effort to secure the honest observance of the law. . . .

*"The Puritan Spirit and the Regulation of
Corporations," address at the laying of the
cornerstone of the Pilgrim Memorial
Monument, Provincetown, Massachusetts,
August 20, 1907*

Every time a big moneyed offender, who naturally excites interest and sympathy, and who has many friends, is excused from serving a sentence, which a man of less prominence and fewer friends would have to serve, justice is discredited in the eyes of plain people—and to undermine faith in justice is to strike at the foundation of the Republic.

Autobiography, 1913

The Man in the Arena

It is not the critic who counts; not the man who points out how the strong man stumbles, or where the doer of deeds could have done them better. The credit belongs to the man who is actually in the arena, whose face is marred by dust and sweat and blood; who strives valiantly; who errs and comes up short again and again, because there is no effort without error or shortcoming; but who does actually strive to do the deeds; who knows the great enthusiasms, the great devotions; who spends himself in a worthy cause; who at the best knows in the end the triumph of high achievement, and who at the worst, if he fails, at least fails while daring greatly, so that his place shall never be with those cold timid souls who know neither victory nor defeat.

"Citizenship in a Republic," speech at
the Sorbonne, Paris, April 23, 1910

Manhood

We need then the iron qualities that must go with true manhood. We need the positive virtues of resolution, of courage, of indomitable will, of power to do without shirking the rough work that must always be done, and to persevere through the long days of slow progress or of seeming failure which always come before any final triumph, no matter how brilliant.

"Manhood and Statehood," address at the
Quarter-Centennial Celebration of Statehood
in Colorado, Colorado Springs,
August 2, 1891

The Medal of Honor
I am entitled to the Medal of Honor, and I want it.
> *TR to Henry Cabot Lodge, December 1, 1898,*
> *Letters*

Military Service
There is no more possibility of a draft or of any serious burden of military service in this country than there is a possibility of George III's coming to life again; and the man who proposes to feel frightened about the one might as well express nervousness as to the possibility of the other.
> *"The Prophecies of Mr. Bryan," speech at*
> *Detroit, Michigan, September 7, 1900*

So far as self-defense is concerned, universal military training, and in the event of need, universal military service, represents the highest expression of the democratic ideal in government.
> *"Where There Is a Sword for Offense, There*
> *Must Be a Sword for Defense," Fear God*
> *and Take Your Own Part, 1916*

Monopoly
All business into which the element of monopoly in any way or degree enters, and where it proves in practice impossible totally to eliminate this element of monopoly, should be carefully supervised, regulated, and controlled by governmental authority; and such control should be exercised by administrative, rather than by judicial, officers.
> *"A Charter of Democracy," address before*
> *the Ohio Constitutional Convention at*
> *Columbus, Ohio, February 21, 1912*

The Monroe Doctrine
The Monroe Doctrine is not a question of law at all. It is a question of policy. . . . The Monroe Doctrine may be briefly

defined as forbidding European encroachment on American soil. . . . The United States has not the slightest wish to establish a universal protectorate over other American States, or to become responsible for their misdeeds. If one of them becomes involved in an ordinary quarrel with a European power, such quarrel must be settled between them by any one of the usual methods. But no European State is to be allowed to aggrandize itself on American soil at the expense of any American State. Furthermore, no transfer of an American colony from one European State to another is to be permitted, if, in the judgment of the United States, such transfer would be hostile to its own interests.
"The Monroe Doctrine," The Bachelor of Arts,
March 1896

The United States ought not to permit any great military powers, which have no foothold on this continent, to establish such foothold; nor should they permit any aggrandizement of those who already have possessions on the continent.
Ibid.

I regard the Monroe Doctrine as being equivalent to the open door in South America. That is, I do not want the United States or any European power to get territorial possessions in South America but to let South America gradually develop on its own lines, with an open door to all outside nations, save as the individual countries enter into individual treaties with one another. Of course this would not anywhere interfere with transitory intervention on the part of any State outside of South America, when there was a row with some State in South America. I wish that the same policy could be pursued in China. That is, the Chinese could be forced to behave themselves—not permitted to do anything atrocious, but not partitioned, and with the ports kept open to all comers, as well as having the vexatious

trade restrictions which prevent inter-Chinese trade in the interior, abolished.
    TR to Hermann Speck von Sternberg,
    October 11, 1901, Letters

We hold that our interests in this hemisphere are greater than those of any European power possibly can be, and that our duty to ourselves and to the weaker republics who are our neighbors requires us to see that none of the great military powers from across the seas shall encroach upon the territory of the American republics or acquire control thereover.

This policy, therefore, not only forbids us to acquiesce in such territorial acquisition, but also causes us to object to the acquirement of a control which would in its effect be equal to territorial aggrandizement.
    "The Monroe Doctrine," speech at Chicago,
    Illinois, April 2, 1903

The Monroe Doctrine is not international law, and though I think one day it may become such, this is not necessary as long as it remains a cardinal feature of our foreign policy and as long as we possess both the will and the strength to make it effective.
    Ibid.

South of the Equator, that is, south of the line of approaches on each side to the Panama Canal, we need no longer bother about the Monroe Doctrine. Brazil, Chile, the Argentine, are capable themselves of handling the Monroe Doctrine for all South America, excepting the extreme northern part. . . . We need bother with the Monroe Doctrine only so far as the approaches to the Panama Canal are concerned. . . . We do not have to bother about the Monroe Doctrine and Canada. . . .
    "Uncle Sam's Only Friend Is Uncle Sam,"
    Metropolitan, November 1915

Mothers and Motherhood

Alone of human beings the good and wise mother stands on a plane of equal honor with the bravest soldier; for she has gladly gone down to the brink of the chasm of darkness to bring back the children in whose hands rests the future of the years.

> *The Great Adventure, 1918*

Muckrakers

There should be relentless exposure of and attack upon every evil man whether politician or business man, every evil practice, whether in politics, in business, or in social life. I hail as a benefactor every writer or speaker, every man who, on the platform, or in book, magazine, or newspaper, with merciless severity makes such attack, provided always that he in his turn remembers that the attack is of use only if it is absolutely truthful.

> *"The Man with a Muck-rake," address at the*
> *laying of the cornerstone of the office building*
> *of the House of Representatives, April 14, 1906*

An epidemic of indiscriminate assault upon character does not good, but very great harm.

> *Ibid.*

Nature Fakers

I don't believe for a minute that some of these men who are writing nature stories and putting the word "truth" prominently in their prefaces know the heart of the wild things. Neither do I believe that certain men who, while they may say nothing specifically about truth, do claim attention as realists because of their animal stories, have succeeded in learning the real secrets of the life of the wilderness. They don't know, of if they do know, they indulge in the wildest exaggerations under the mistaken notion that they are strengthening their stories.

"Men Who Misinterpret Nature," from an interview with Edward B. Clark in Everybody's Magazine, June 1907

The preservation of the useful and beautiful animal and bird life of the country depends largely upon creating in the young an interest in the life of the wood and fields. If the child mind is fed with stories that are false to nature, the children will go to the haunts of the animal only to meet with disappointment. The result will be disbelief, and the death of interest. The men who misinterpret nature and replace facts with fiction, undo the work of those who in the love of nature interpret it aright.

Ibid.

The modern "nature-faker" is of course an object of derision to every scientist worthy of the name, to every real lover of the wilderness, to every faunal naturalist, to every true hunter or nature-lover.

"Nature-Fakers," Everybody's Magazine, September 1907

We who believe in the study of nature feel that a real knowledge and appreciation of wild things, of trees, flowers, birds, and of the grim and crafty creatures of the wildness, give an added beauty and health to life. Therefore we abhor deliberate or reckless untruth in this study as much as in any other; and therefore we feel that a grave wrong is committed by all who, holding a position that entitles them to respect, yet condone and encourage such untruth.

Ibid.

The Negro

The difference between what can and what cannot be done by law is well exemplified by our experience with the negro problem. . . . The negroes were formerly held in slavery. This was a wrong which legislation could remedy, and which could not be remedied except by legislation. Accordingly they were set free by law. This having been done, many of their friends believed that in some way, by additional legislation, we could at once put them on an intellectual, social, and business equality with the whites. The effort has failed completely. In large sections of the country the negroes are not treated as they should be treated, and politically in particular the frauds upon them have been so gross and shameful as to awaken not merely indignation but bitter wrath; yet the best friends of the negro admit that his hope lies, not in legislation, but in constant working of those often unseen forces of the national life which are greater than all legislation.

"How Not to Help Our Poorer Brother,"
Review of Reviews, January 1897

As a people striving to shape our actions in accordance with the great law of righteousness we cannot afford to take part in or be indifferent to the oppression or maltreatment of any man who, against crushing disadvantages, has by his own industry, energy, self-respect, and perseverance struggled upward to a position which would entitle him to the respect of his fellows, if only his skin were of a different hue.

Every generous impulse in us revolts at the thought of thrusting down instead of helping up such a man. To deny any man the fair treatment granted to others no better than he is to commit a wrong upon him—a wrong sure to react in the long run upon those guilty of such denial. The only safe principle upon which Americans can act is that of "all men up," not that of "some men down."

"The Negro Problem," address at the
Lincoln Dinner of the Republican Club of the
City of New York, February 13, 1905

We feel with all our hearts that in a democracy like ours, and, above all, in such a genuinely democratic movement as ours, we cannot permanently succeed except on the basis of treating each man on his worth as a man. The humblest among us, no matter what his creed, his birthplace, or the color of his skin, so long as he behaves in straight and decent fashion, must have guaranteed to him under the law his right to life and liberty, to protection from injustice, to the enjoyment of the fruits of his own labor, and to do his share in the work of self-government on the same terms with others of like fitness. Our movement is in the interest of every honest, industrious, law-abiding colored man, just as it is in the interest of every honest, industrious, law-abiding white man. To this cause, embodying this as one of our chief tenets, we have dedicated ourselves, with whatever of high purpose, of wisdom, patience, and resolute courage we possess.

"The Progressive and the Colored Man,"
The Outlook, August 24, 1912

Neutrality

It is not a lofty thing, on the contrary it is an evil thing, to practice a timid and selfish neutrality between right and wrong. It is wrong for an individual. It is still more wrong for a nation. But it is worse in the name of neutrality to favor the nation that has done evil.

"This Nation's Needs," address at Plattsburgh,
New York, August 25, 1915

New Amsterdam

The Europeans who came to this city during its forty years of life represented almost every grade of Old World society. Many of these pioneers were men of as high character and standing as ever took part in founding a new settlement; but on the other hand there were plenty of others to the full as vicious and worthless as the worst immigrants who have come hither during the present century. Many imported bond servants and apprentices, both English and Irish, of criminal **or** semicriminal tendencies escaped to Manhattan from Virginia and from New England, and, once here, found congenial associates from half the countries of continental Europe. Thus there existed from the start a low, shiftless, evil class of whites in our population while even beneath their squalid ranks lay the herd of brutalized black slaves. It may be questioned whether seventeenth-century New Amsterdam did not include quite as large a proportion of undesirable inhabitants as nineteen-century New York.

New York, 1660–1890 (1891)

New York and New Yorkers

The history of New York deserves to be studied for more than one reason. It is the history of the largest English-speaking city which the English conquered but did not found, and in which though the English law and governmental system have ever been supreme, yet the bulk of the population, composed as it is and ever has been of many shifting strains, has never been English. Again, for the past hundred years, it is the history of a wonderfully prosperous trading city, the largest in the world in which the democratic plan has ever been faithfully tried for so long a time; and the trial, made under some exceptional advantages and some equally exceptional disadvantages, is of immense interest, alike for the measure in which it has succeeded and for the measure in which it has failed.

New York, 1660–1890 (1891)

With many very serious shortcomings and defects, the average New Yorker yet possesses courage, energy, business capacity, much generosity of a practical sort, and shrewd, humorous common sense.

Ibid.

Nostrums

Quack remedies of the universal cure-all type are generally as noxious to the body politic as to the body corporal.

"How Not to Help Our Poorer Brother,"
Review of Reviews, January 1897

Distrust whoever pretends to offer you a patent cure-all for every ill of the body politic, just as you would a man who offers a medicine which would cure every evil of your individual body. A medicine that is recommended to cure both asthma and a broken leg is not good for either.

"The Control of Corporations," address at
Providence, Rhode Island, August 23, 1903

Opportunity

But it remains true that, in spite of all our faults and shortcomings, no other land offers such glorious possibilities to the man able to take advantage of them, as does ours; it remains true that no one of our people can do any work really worth doing unless he does it primarily as an American.

"True Americanism," The Forum, April 1894

It is of the utmost importance that in the future we shall keep the broad path of opportunity just as open and easy for our children as it was for our fathers during the period

which has been the glory of America's industrial history—
that it shall be not only possible but easy for an ambitious
man, whose character has so impressed itself upon his
neighbors that they are willing to give him capital and
credit, to start in business for himself, and, if his superior efficiency deserves it, to triumph over the biggest organization that may happen to exist in his particular field.
Whatever practices upon the part of large combinations
may threaten to discourage such a man, or deny to him that
which in the judgment of the community is a square deal,
should be specifically defined by the statutes as crimes.
And in every case the individual corporation officer responsible for such unfair dealing should be punished.

> *"A Charter of Democracy," address before
> the Ohio Constitutional Convention at
> Columbus, Ohio, February 21, 1912*

Pacifists and Pacifism

A class of professional noncombatants is as hurtful to the
healthy growth of a nation as a class of fire-eaters, for a
weakness or folly is nationally as bad as a vice, or worse.
No man who is not willing to bear arms and to fight for his
rights can give a good reason why he should be entitled to
the privilege of living in a free country.

> *Life of William Hart Benton, 1887*

Probably no body of citizens in the United States during the
last five years have wrought so efficient for national decadence and international degradation as the professional
pacifists, the peace-at-any-price men, who have tried to
teach our people that silly all inclusive arbitration treaties
and the utterance of fatuous platitudes at peace congresses
are [a] substitute for adequate military preparedness.

> *"This Nation's Needs," address at Plattsburgh,
> New York, August 25, 1915*

Both the professional pacifists and the professional hyphenated American need to be taught that it is not for them to decide the conditions under which they will fight. They will fight whoever the nation decides to fight, and whenever the nation deems a war necessary.

Ibid.

Panama Canal

The great bit of work of my administration, and from the material and constructive standpoint, one of the greatest bits of work that the twentieth century will see, is the Isthmian Canal. . . .

TR to John Hay, July 1, 1902, Letters

Why cannot we buy the Panama isthmus outright instead of leasing it from Colombia? It seems to be a very good thing. I think they would change their constitution if we offered enough.

TR to John Hay, August 21, 1902, Letters

To my mind this building of the canal through Panama will rank in kind, though not of course in degree, with the Louisiana purchase and the acquisition of Texas. I can say with entire conscientiousness that if in order to get the treaty through and start building the canal it were necessary for me forthwith to retire definitely from politics, I should be only too glad to make the arrangement accordingly; for it is the amount done in office, and not length of time in office, that makes office worth having.

TR to Samuel White Small, December 29, 1903, Letters

I have succeeded in accomplishing a certain amount which I think will stand. I believe I shall put through the Panama treaty (my worst foes being those in the Senate and not those outside of the borders of the United States) and begin to dig the canal. . . . The people of the United States and the people of the Isthmus and the rest of mankind will all be the better because we dig the Panama Canal and keep order in the neighborhood. And the politicians and revolutionists at Bogota are entitled to precisely the amount of sympathy we extend to other inefficient bandits.

> *TR to Cecil Arthur Spring Rice,*
> *January 18, 1904, Letters*

The Panama Canal I naturally take special interest in because I started it. [*Laughter and applause.*]

There are plenty of other things I started merely because the time had come that whoever was in power would have started them.

But the Panama Canal would not have been started if I had not taken hold of it, because if I had followed the traditional or conservative method I should have submitted an admirable state paper occupying a couple of hundred pages detailing all of the facts to Congress and asking Congress' consideration of it.

In that case there would have been a number of excellent speeches made on the subject in Congress; the debate would be proceeding at this moment with great spirit and the beginning of work on the canal would be fifty years in the future. [*Laughter and applause.*]

Fortunately the crisis came at a period when I could act unhampered. Accordingly I took the Isthmus, started the canal and then left Congress not to debate the canal, but to debate me. [*Laughter and applause.*]

> *Speech at Berkeley, California, March 31, 1911*

Party Loyalty

The average man is a Democrat or a Republican and he is this as a matter of faith, not as a matter of morals. He no

more requires a reason for so being than an adherent of the blue or green factions of the Byzantine Circus required a reason. He has grown to accept as co-relative to this attitude entire willingness to punish his party by voting for the opposite party. Having done this, he returns to his own party.
> *TR to Charles J. Bonaparte, November 7, 1914,*
> *Letters*

Patriotism
The man who loves other countries as much as he does his own is quite as noxious a member of society as the man who loves other women as much as he loves his wife.
> *"The Monroe Doctrine," The Bachelor of Arts,*
> *March 1896*

The man who loves other nations as much as he does his own, stands on a par with the man who loves other women as much as he does his own wife.
> *Fear God and Take Your Own Part, 1916*

The man who feels that the country owes him everything and that he owes the country nothing, will pay the country just what he thinks he owes—nothing.
> *"The Children of the Crucible," in The Foes of*
> *Our Own Household, 1917*

Peace
Peace is a goddess only when she comes with sword girt on thigh.
> *"Washington's Forgotten Maxim," address*
> *before the Naval War College, Newport,*
> *Rhode Island, June 2, 1897*

Remember that peace itself, that peace after which all men crave, is merely the realization in the present of what has been bought by strenuous effort in the past. Peace represents stored-up effort of our fathers or of ourselves in the past. It is not a means—it is an end. You do not get peace by peace; you get peace as the result of effort. If you strive to get it by peace you will lose it, that is all.

> *"America's Part of the World's Work," address*
> *at the Lincoln Club Dinner in New York City,*
> *February 13, 1899*

We sincerely and earnestly believe in peace; but if peace and justice conflict, we scorn the man who would not stand for justice though the whole world came in arms against him.

> *"Citizenship in a Republic," speech at the*
> *Sorbonne, Paris, April 23, 1910*

When I left the presidency, I finished seven and a half years of administration, during which not one shot had been fired against a foreign foe. We were at absolute peace, and there was no nation in the world whom we had wronged, or from whom we had anything to fear.

> *Autobiography, 1913*

Play

Play while you play and work while you work; and though play is a mighty good thing, remember that you had better never play at all than to get into a condition of mind where you regard play as the serious business of life, or where you permit it to hamper and interfere with your doing your full duty in the real work of the world.

> *"Athletics, Scholarship, and Public Service,"*
> *address at the Harvard Union, Cambridge,*
> *Massachusetts, February 23, 1907*

Politics

If you look up the correspondence about the original appointments of Messrs. Wimberly and Sauer, you will find

that they were engaged in a ferocious factional fight of the usual reputable southern professional politician type, and that each accused the other of crimes, which if one-tenth true warranted the imprisonment of both. They then came together and cordially recommended each other for office.
    TR to Henry Clay Payne, July 8, 1902, Letters

Preparedness
Preparation for war is the surest guaranty for peace. Arbitration is an excellent thing, but ultimately those who wish to see this country at peace with foreign nations will be wise if they place reliance upon a first-class fleet of first-class battleships. . . .
    "Washington's Forgotten Maxim," address
    before the Naval War College, Newport,
    Rhode Island, June 2, 1897

An unmanly desire to avoid a quarrel is often the surest way to precipitate one; and utter unreadiness to fight is even surer.
    Ibid.

I suppose the United States will always be unready for war, and in consequence will always be exposed to great expense, and to the possibility of the gravest calamity, when the Nation goes to war. This is no new thing. Americans learn only from catastrophes and not from experience.
    Autobiography, 1913

All our young men should be trained so that at need they can fight. Under the conditions of modern warfare it is the wildest nonsense to talk of men springing to arms in mass unless they have been taught how to act and how to use the arms to which they spring.
    "This Nation's Needs," address at Plattsburgh,
    New York, August 25, 1915

No man is fit to be free unless he is not merely willing but eager to fit himself to fight for his freedom, and no man can fight for his freedom unless he is trained to act in conjunction with his fellows. The worst of all feelings to arouse in others is the feeling of contempt. Those men have mean souls who desire that this nation shall not be fit to defend its own rights and that its sons shall not possess a high and resolute temper. But even men of stout heart need to remember that when the hour for action has struck no courage will avail unless there has been thorough training, thorough preparation in advance.

> *Ibid.*

The President

The candidate is the candidate of a party; but if the President is worth his salt he is the President of the whole people. Remember, the stream does not rise any higher than its source.

> *Speech at City Park, Little Rock, Arkansas,*
> *October 25, 1905*

Not only do I myself believe, but I am firmly convinced that the great mass of the American people believe, that when the President leaves public office he should become exactly like any other man in private life. He is entitled to no privileges; but on the other hand, he is also entitled to be treated no worse than any one else.

> *TR to Melville E. Stone, December 2, 1908,*
> *Letters*

To announce that there must be no criticism of the President, or that we are to stand by the President, right or wrong, is not only unpatriotic and servile, but is morally treasonable to the American public. Nothing but the truth should be spoken about him or any one else. But it is even more important to tell the truth, pleasant or unpleasant, about him than about any one else.

"Lincoln and Free Speech,"
in The Great Adventure, 1918

Presidential Power

The most important factor in getting the right spirit in my Administration, next to the insistence upon courage, honesty, and a genuine democracy of desire to serve the plain people, was my insistence upon the theory that the executive power was limited only by specific restrictions and prohibitions appearing in the Constitution or imposed by the Congress under its Constitutional powers. My view was that every executive officer, and above all every executive officer in high position, was steward of the people bound actively and affirmatively to do all he could for the people, and not to content himself with the negative merit of keeping his talents undamaged in a napkin. I declined to adopt the view that what was imperatively necessary for the Nation could not be done by the President unless he could find some specific authorization to do it. My belief was that it was not only his right but his duty to do anything that the needs of the Nation demanded unless such action was forbidden by the Constitution or by the laws. Under this interpretation of executive power I did and caused to be done many things not previously done by the President and the heads of the departments. I did not usurp power, but I did greatly broaden the use of executive power. In other words, I acted for the public welfare, I acted for the common well-being of all our people, whenever and in whatever manner was necessary, unless prevented by direct constitutional or legislative prohibition. I did not care a rap for the mere form and show of power; I cared immensely for the use that could be made of the substance.

Autobiography, 1913

In every such crisis the temptation to indecision, to non-action, is great, for excuses can always be found for non-action, and action means risk and the certainty of blame to the man who acts. But if the man is worth his salt he will do his duty, he will give people the benefit of the doubt, and act in any way which their interests demand which is not affirmatively prohibited by law, unheeding the likelihood that he himself, when the crisis is over and the danger past, will be assailed for what he has done.

Ibid.

Property

The true conservative is he who insists that property shall be the servant and not the master of the commonwealth.

"The New Nationalism," speech at Osawatomie, Kansas, August 31, 1910

We are face to face with new conceptions of the relations of property to human welfare, chiefly because certain advocates of the rights of property as against the rights of men have been pushing their claims too far. The man who wrongly holds that every human right is secondary to his profit must now give way to the advocate of human welfare, who rightly maintains that every man holds his property subject to the general right of the community to regulate its use to whatever degree the public welfare may require it.

Ibid.

Public Service

Like most young men in politics, I went through various oscillations of feeling before I "found myself." At one period I became so impressed with the virtue of complete independence that I proceeded to act on each case purely as I personally viewed it, without paying any heed to the principles and prejudices of others. The result was that I speedily and deservedly lost all power of accomplishing anything at all; and I thereby learned the invaluable lesson that in the practical activities of life no man can render the highest service unless he can act in combination with his fellows, which means a certain amount of give-and-take between him and them. Again, I at one period began to believe that I had a future before me, and that it behooved me to be very far-sighted and scan each action carefully with a view to its possible effect on that future. This speedily made me useless to the public and an object of aversion to myself; and I then made up my mind that I would try not to think of the future at all, but would proceed on the assumption that each office I held would be the last I ever should hold, and that I would confine myself to trying to do my work as well as possible while I held that office. I found that for me personally this was the only way in which I could either enjoy myself or render good service to the country, and I never afterwards deviated from this plan.

Autobiography, 1913

Reform and Reformers
It is contemptible to oppose a movement for good because that movement has already succeeded somewhere else, or to champion an existing abuse because our people have always been wedded to it. To appeal to national prejudice against a given reform movement is in every way unworthy and silly.

"True Americanism," The Forum, April 1894

Now, gentlemen, don't be content with mere effervescent denunciation of one thing or another. Evil can't be done away with through one spasm of virtue.

Speech at the City Club, New York City,
May 9, 1899

The men with the muck-rakes are often indispensable to the well-being of society; but only if they know when to stop raking the muck, and to look upward to the celestial crown above them, to the crown of worthy endeavor.

"The Man with the Muck-rake," address
at the laying of the cornerstone of the
office building of the House of Representatives,
Washington, D.C., April 14, 1906

Religion
The claims of certain so-called scientific men as to "science overthrowing religion" are as baseless as the fears of certain sincerely religious men on the same subject. The establishment of the doctrine of evolution in our time offers no more justification for upsetting religious beliefs than the discovery of the facts concerning the solar system a few centuries ago. Any faith sufficiently robust to stand the— surely very slight—strain of admitting that the world is not flat and does move round the sun need have no apprehensions on the score of evolution, and the materialistic scientists who gleefully hail the discovery of the principle of evolution as establishing their dreary creed might with just as much propriety rest it upon the discovery of the principle of gravitation.

"The Search for Truth in a Reverent Spirit,"
The Outlook, December 2, 1911

We must all strive to keep as our most precious heritage the liberty each has to worship his God as to him seems best, and, as part of this liberty, freely either to exercise it or to surrender it, in a greater or less degree, each according to his own beliefs and convictions, without infringing on the beliefs and convictions of others.

Ibid.

I hold that in this country there must be complete severance of Church and State; that public moneys shall not be used for the purpose of advancing any particular creed; and therefore that the public schools shall be non-sectarian and no public moneys appropriated for sectarian schools. As a necessary corollary to this, not only the pupils but the members of the teaching force and the school officials of all kinds must be treated exactly on a par, no matter what their creed; and there must be no more discrimination against Jew or Catholic or Protestant than discrimination in favor of Jew, Catholic, or Protestant. Whoever makes such discrimination is an enemy of the public schools.

> *"Americanism," Address before the Knights of*
> *Columbus, Carnegie Hall, New York,*
> *October 12, 1915; in Fear God and*
> *Take Your Own Part, 1916*

Alice Roosevelt

I can govern the United States or I can govern my daughter, Alice, but I can't do both.

> *Attributed to TR in Wister*

Roosevelt on Roosevelt

So, Kermit, we shall know nothing about the result until the votes [of the presidential election of 1904] are counted, and in the meanwhile must possess our souls in patience. If things go wrong remember that we are very, very fortunate to have had three years in the White House, and that I have had a chance to accomplish work such as comes to very, very few men in any generation; and that I have no business to feel downcast or querulous merely because when so much has been given me I have not had even more.

> *TR to Kermit Roosevelt, October 26, 1904,*
> *Letters*

I am still looking forward, not back. I do not know any man who has had as happy a fifty years as I have had. I have had about as good a run for my money as any human being possibly could have; and whatever happens now I am ahead of the game.

> TR to Frederic Remington, October, 28, 1908,
> Letters

I am not in the least a hero, my dear fellow. I am a perfectly commonplace man and I know it; I am just a decent American citizen who tries to stand for what is decent in his own country and in other countries and who owes very much to you and to certain men like you who are not fellow-countrymen of his.

> TR to George Otto Trevelyan, May 29, 1915,
> Letters

I have only a second-rate brain, but I think I have a capacity for action.

> Quoted in Owen Wister, Theodore Roosevelt:
> The Story of a Friendship, 1930

Russia and the Russians

If Russia chooses to develop purely on her own line and to resist the growth of liberalism, then she may put off the day of reckoning; but she cannot ultimately avert it, and instead of occasionally having to go through what Kansas has gone through with the Populists, *she will some time experience a red terror which will make the French Revolution pale.* [TR's italics]

> TR to Cecil Arthur Spring Rice,
> August 11, 1898, Letters

For several years Russia has behaved very badly in the far East, her attitude toward all nations, including us, but especially toward Japan, being grossly overbearing. We had not sufficient cause for war with her. Yet I was apprehensive lest if she at the very outset whipped Japan on the sea she might assume a position well-nigh intolerable toward us. I thought Japan would probably whip her on the sea, but I could not be certain; and between ourselves—for you must not breathe it to anybody—I was thoroughly well pleased with the Japanese victory, for Japan is playing our game.

TR to Theodore Roosevelt Junior,
February 10, 1904, Letters

I frankly admire the Russian people and I wish them well. Moreover, I have never been able to make myself afraid of them, because it has always seemed to me that a despotism resting upon a corrupt and to a large extent an incapable bureaucracy could not in the long run be dangerous to a virile free people. The average man who speaks English can outwork, outadminister, outthink and outfight the average Russian; and this will be true until the average Russian grows to have more liberty, more self-respect and more intelligence than at present.

TR to George Trevelyan, September 12, 1905,
Letters

Scholarship
From the standpoint of the nation, and from the broader standpoint of mankind, scholarship is of worth chiefly when it is productive, when the scholar not merely receives or acquires, but gives.

"Productive Scholarship," The Outlook,
January 13, 1912

Seeing
Most big-game hunters never learn anything about the game except how to kill it; and most naturalists never observe it at all. Therefore a large amount of important and rather obvious facts remain unobserved or inaccurately observed until the species becomes extinct. What is most

needed is not the ability to see what very few people can see, but to see what almost anybody can see, but nobody takes the trouble to look at.

"My Life as a Naturalist," American
Museum Journal, May 1918

Self-Government

The great fundamental issue now before the Republican Party and before our people can be stated briefly. It is, Are the American people fit to govern themselves, to rule themselves, to control themselves? I believe they are. My opponents do not. I believe in the right of people to rule. I believe the majority of the plain people of the United States will, day in and day out, make fewer mistakes in governing themselves than any smaller class or body of men, no matter what their training, will make in trying to govern them. I believe, again, that the American people are, as a whole, capable of self-control and of learning by their mistakes. Our opponents pay lip-loyalty to this doctrine; but they show their real beliefs by the way in which they champion every device to make the nominal rule of the people a sham.

"The Right of the People to Rule," address at
Carnegie Hall, New York City, March 20, 1912

Self-Reliance

The worst lesson that can be taught a man is to rely upon others and to whine over his sufferings. If an American is to amount to anything he must rely upon himself, and not upon the State; he must take pride in his own work, instead of sitting idle to envy the luck of others; he must face life with resolute courage, win victory if he can, and accept defeat if he must, without seeking to place on his fellow-men a responsibility which is not theirs.

"How Not to Help Our Poorer Brother,"
Review of Reviews, January 1897

[I]t is both foolish and wicked to teach the average man who is not well off that some wrong or injustice has been done him, and that he should hope for redress elsewhere than in his own industry, honesty, and intelligence.
Ibid.

If a man stumbles, it is a good thing to help him to his feet. Every one of us needs a helping hand now and then. But if a man lies down, it is a waste of time to try to carry him; and it is a very bad thing for every one if we make men feel that the same reward will come to those who shirk their work and to those who do it.
*"Citizenship in a Republic," speech at
the Sorbonne, Paris, April 23, 1910*

The Senate
The last time I saw poor John Hay I told him that the more I saw of the Czar and the Kaiser the better I liked the United States Senate; to which he was evidently inclined to respond that he drew no fine distinctions between them. It is evident that the Senate is a very poor body to have as part of the treaty-making power.
*TR to Cecil Arthur Spring Rice, July 24, 1905,
Letters*

There are in the Senate, perhaps half a dozen, but probably only two or three, doctrinaires, who on academic lines are sincerely doubtful about the [Santo Domingo] treaty; that is, there is about the same proportion of off oxen as you find in any average body of men on any subject.
*TR to Lincoln Steffens, February 6, 1906,
Letters*

In this nation, as in any nation which amounts to anything, those in the end must govern who are willing actually to do the work of governing; and in so far as the Senate becomes a mere obstructionist body it will run the risk of seeing its power pass into other hands.

TR to John St. Loe Strachey, February 12, 1906, Letters

Settlers

The warlike borderers who thronged across the Alleghanies, the restless and reckless hunters, the hard dogged, frontier farmers, by dint of grim tenacity, overcame and displaced Indians, French, and Spaniards alike, exactly as, fourteen hundred years before, Saxon and Angle had overcome and displaced the Cymric and Gaelic Celts. They were led by no one commander; they acted under orders from neither king nor congress; they were not carrying out the plans of any far-sighted leader. In obedience to the instincts working half blindly within their breasts, spurred ever onward by the fierce desires of their eager hearts, they made in the wilderness homes for their children, and by so doing wrought out the destinies of a continental nation. . . . They were doing their share of a work that began with the conquest of Britain, that entered on its second and wider period after the defeat of the Spanish Armada, that culminated in the marvelous growth of the United States. The winning of the West and Southwest is a stage in the conquest of a continent.

The Winning of the West, 1889

Snobbery

Every now and then I meet . . . the man who having gone through college feels that somehow that confers upon him a special distinction which relieves him from the necessity of showing himself as good as his fellows. . . . That man is not only a curse to the community, and incidentally to himself, but he is a curse to the cause of academic education, the college and university training, because by his insistence he serves as an excuse for those who like to denounce such education. Your education, your training, will not confer on you one privilege in the way of excusing you from effort or from work. All it can do, and what it should do, is to make you a little better fitted for such effort, for such work. . . .

Address at Leland Stanford, Junior, University,
Palo Alto, California, May 12, 1903

I have grown to have a constantly increasing horror of the Americans who go abroad desiring to be presented at court or to meet sovereigns. In very young people it is excusable folly; in older people it is mere snobbishness.

TR to Whitelaw Reid, May 25, 1908, Letters

The Spoils System

I think that, of all people who are harmed by the spoils system, the poor suffer most. The rich man who wishes to corrupt a legislature, or the rich company which wishes to buy franchises from a board of aldermen and pay a big price for it, do not suffer so much as the poor from the results of the system. I dare say that in New York we see the system at its worst, but at its best it is thoroughly rotten, and a disgrace to every community enjoying the right of suffrage.

"The Spoils System in Operation," speech at the
meeting of the Civil Service Reform Association,
Baltimore, Maryland, February 23, 1889

A Square Deal

A man who is good enough to shed his blood for his country is good enough to be given a square deal afterwards.

Life of Thomas Hart Benton, 1887

All I ask is a square deal for every man. Give him a fair chance. Do not let him wrong any one, and do not let him be wronged.

Speech at the Grand Canyon, May 6, 1903

It is a good thing that the guard around the tomb of Lincoln should be composed of colored soldiers. It was my own good fortune at Santiago to serve beside colored troops. A man who is good enough to shed his blood for his country is good enough to be given a square deal afterwards. More than that no man is entitled to, and less than that no man shall have.

> *Speech at the Lincoln Monument,*
> *Springfield, Illinois, June 4, 1903*

We must treat each man on his worth and merits as a man. We must see that each is given a square deal, because he is entitled to no more and should receive no less.

> *"National Unity versus Class Cleavage,"*
> *Labor Day address at New York State Fair,*
> *Syracuse, New York, September 7, 1903*

When I say I believe in a square deal I do not mean, and no-body who speaks the truth can mean, that he believes it possible to give every man the best hand. If the cards do not come to any man, of if they do come, and he has not got the power to play them, that is his affair. All I mean is that there shall not be any crookedness in the dealing. In other words, it is not in the power of any human being to devise legislation or administration by which each man shall achieve success and have happiness. . . .

> *Speech at Dallas, Texas, April 5, 1905*

We demand that big business give the people a square deal; in return we must insist that when anyone engaged in big business honestly endeavors to do right he shall himself be given a square deal.

> *TR to Sir Edward Grey, November 15, 1913, Letters*

A square deal for every man! That is the only safe motto for the United States.

> *TR to Victor A. Olander, July 17, 1917, quoted in "Murder Is Not Debatable," open letter, July 20, 1917*

The Stars and Stripes

We have room in this country for but one flag, the Stars and Stripes, and we should tolerate no allegiance to any other flag, whether a foreign flag or the red flag or black flag.

> *"The Square Deal in Americanism," Metropolitan, February, August 1918; in The Great Adventure, 1918*

States' Rights

It [the Republican party] remained the Nationalist as against the particularist or State's [sic] rights party, and in so far it remained absolutely sound; for little permanent good can be done by any party which worships the State's rights fetish or which fails to regard the State, like the country or the municipality, as merely a convenient unit for local self-government, while in all National matters, of importance to the whole people, the Nation is to be supreme over State, county, and town alike. But the State's rights fetish, although still effectively used at certain times by both courts and Congress to block needed National legislation directed against the huge corporations or in the interests of workingmen, was not a prime issue at the time of which I speak. . . .

> *Autobiography, 1913*

Statesmanship

It is the duty of wise statesmen, gifted with power of looking ahead, to try to encourage and build up every movement which will substitute or tend to substitute some other agency for force in the settlement of international disputes.

*"Citizenship in a Republic," speech at
the Sorbonne, Paris, April 23, 1910*

The Strenuous Life
I wish to preach, not the doctrine of ignoble ease, but the doctrine of the strenuous life, the life of toil and effort, of labor and strife; to preach that highest form of success which comes, not to the man who desires mere easy peace, but to the man who does not shrink from danger, from hardship, or from bitter toil and who out of these wins the splendid ultimate triumph.

A life of slothful ease, a life of that peace which springs merely from lack either of desire or of power to strive after great things, is as little worthy of a nation as of an individual.

*"The Strenuous Life," speech before the
Hamilton Club, Chicago, April 10, 1899*

In short, in life, as in a foot-ball game, the principle to follow is: Hit the line hard; don't foul and don't shirk, but hit the line hard!

"The American Boy," St. Nicholas, May 1900

The life that is worth living, and the only life that is worth living, is the life of effort, the life of effort to attain what is worth striving for.

*"The Journey on the Ridge Crest," speech at
the Prize-Day Exercises at Groton School,
May 24, 1904*

I once made a speech to which I gave the title "The Strenuous Life." Afterwards I published a volume of essays with this for a title. There were two translations of it which

always especially pleased me. One was by a Japanese officer who knew English well, and who had carried the essay
all through the Manchurian campaign, and later translated
it for the benefit of his countrymen. The other was by an
Italian lady, whose brother, an officer in the Italian army
who had died on duty in a foreign land, had also greatly
liked the article and carried it round with him. In translat-
ing the title the lady rendered it in Italian as *Vigor di Vita*. I
thought this translation a great improvement on the original, and have always wished that I had myself used "The
Vigor of Life" as a heading to indicate what I was trying to
preach, instead of the heading I actually did use.
        Autobiography, 1913

Success
It is hard to fail, but it is worse never to have tried to succeed.
        "The Strenuous Life," address before
        the Hamilton Club at Chicago, Illinois,
        April 10, 1899

There are two kinds of success. One is the very rare kind
that comes to the man who has the power to do what no
one else has the power to do. That is genius. I am not discussing what form that genius takes; whether it is the genius of a man who can write a poem that no one else can
write, "The Ode on a Grecian Urn," for example, or "Helen,
thy beauty is to me"; or of a man who can do one hundred
yards in nine and three-fifths seconds. Such a man does
what no one else can do. Only a very limited amount of the
success of life comes to persons possessing genius. The average man who is successful—the average statesman, the
average public servant, the average soldier, who wins what
we call great success—is not a genius. He is a man who has

merely the ordinary qualities that he shares with his fellows, but who has developed those ordinary qualities to a more than ordinary degree.
> *"The Conditions of Success," address at*
> *Cambridge University, Cambridge, England,*
> *May 26, 1910*

I thoroughly believe that success—the real success—does not depend upon the position you hold, but upon how you carry yourself in that position.
> *Ibid.*

Any man who has met with success, if he will be frank with himself, must admit that there has been a big element of fortune in the success.
> *Autobiography, 1913*

It is impossible to win the great prizes of life without running risks and the greatest of all prizes are those connected with the home. No father and mother can hope to escape sorrow and anxiety, and there are dreadful moments when death comes very near those we love, even if for the time being it passes by. But life is a great adventure, and the worst of all fears is the fear of living. There are many forms of success, many forms of triumph. But there is no other success that in any shape or way approaches that which is open to most of the many, many men and women who have the right ideals. These are the men and the women who see that it is the intimate and homely things that count most. They are the men and women who have the courage to strive for the happiness which comes only with labor and effort and self-sacrifice, and only to those whose joy in life springs in part from power of work and sense of duty.
> *Ibid.*

The Supreme Court

It seems to me that the head of the Supreme Court should be not merely a learned lawyer but a constructive statesman. It is the failure to understand this fact which has caused certain of the Supreme Court judges to go so lamentably wrong during the past few years.

> *TR to Benjamin Ide Wheeler,*
> *December 12, 1901, Letters*

In the ordinary and low sense which we attach to the words "partisan" and "politician," a judge of the Supreme Court should be neither. But in the higher sense, in the proper sense, he is not in my judgment fitted for the position unless he is a party man, a constructive statesman, constantly keeping in mind his adherence to the principles and policies under which this nation has been built up and in accordance with which it must go on; and keeping in mind also his relations with his fellow statesmen who in other branches of the government are striving in cooperation with him to advance the ends of government.

> *TR to Henry Cabot Lodge, July 10, 1902,*
> *Letters*

Taxes

As a matter of personal conviction, and without pretending to discuss the details or formulate the system, I feel that we shall ultimately have to consider the adoption of some such scheme as that of a progressive tax on all fortunes, beyond a certain amount either given in life or devised or bequeathed upon death to any individual—a tax so framed as to put it out of the power of the owner of one of these enormous fortunes to hand on more than a certain amount to any one individual; the tax, of course, to be imposed by the National and not the State Government. Such taxation should, of course, be aimed merely at the inheritance or transmission in their entirety of those fortunes swollen beyond all healthy limits.

"The Man with the Muck-Rake," address
at the laying of the cornerstone of the
office building of the House of Representatives,
Washington, D.C., April 14, 1906

The really big fortune, the swollen fortune, by the mere fact of its size acquires qualities which differentiate it in kind as well as in degree from what is possessed by men of relatively small means. Therefore, I believe in a graduated income tax on big fortunes, and in another tax which is far more easily collected and far more effective—a graduated inheritance tax on big fortunes, properly safeguarded against evasion and increasing rapidly in amount with the size of the estate.

"The New Nationalism," speech at Osawatomie,
Kansas, August 31, 1910

Tyranny of the Majority
I have scant patience with this talk of the tyranny of the majority. Whenever there is tyranny of the majority, I shall protest against it with all my heart and soul. But we are to-day suffering from the tyranny of minorities. It is a small minority that is grabbing our coal deposits, our water powers, and our harbor fronts. A small minority is battening on the sale of adulterated foods and drugs. It is a small minority that lies behind monopolies and trusts. It is a small minority that stands behind the present law of master and servant, the sweat-shops, and the whole calendar of social and industrial injustice. It is a small minority that is to-day using our convention system to defeat the will of a majority of the people in the choice of delegates to the Chicago Convention.

The only tyrannies from which men, women and children are suffering in real life are the tyrannies of minorities. . . .

Am I overstating the case? Have our political leaders always, or generally, recognized their duty to the people as
anything more than a duty to disperse the mob, see that the
ashes are taken away, and distribute patronage? Have our
leaders always, or generally, worked for the benefit of
human beings, to increase the prosperity of all the people,
to give to each some opportunity of living decently and
bring up his children well? The questions need no answer.

"The Right of the People to Rule," address at
Carnegie Hall, New York City, March 20, 1912

Unions

I believe in labor unions. If I were a wageworker I should
certainly join one; and I am now an honorary member of
one and am very proud of it. But if the members of labor
unions indulge in rioting and violence, or behave wrong-
fully either to a capitalist or to another laborer or to the general public, I shall antagonize them just as fearlessly as
under similar circumstances I should antagonize the
biggest capitalist in the land.

TR to Ray Stannard Baker, August 27, 1904,
Letters

Unpreparedness

We are utterly unprepared. The things we are now doing,
even when well done, are things which we ought to have
begun doing three years ago. We can now only partially offset our folly in failing to prepare during these last three
years, in failing to heed the lesson writ large across the skies
in letters of flame and blood. Nine-tenths of wisdom is
being wise in time. We must fight without proper preparation. . . .

"Nine-Tenths of Wisdom Is Being Wise
in Time," speech at Lincoln, Nebraska,
June 14, 1917

Virtue

To sit at home, read one's favorite paper, and scoff at the misdeeds of the men who do things is easy but is markedly ineffective. It is what evil men count upon the good man's doing; and hitherto there has been this justification for such a belief among bad men—namely, that, as a rule, the corrupt men have been perfectly content to let their opponents monopolize all the virtue while they themselves have been permitted to monopolize all the efficiency.

"The Higher Life of American Cities,"
The Outlook, December 21, 1895

War

The most ultimately righteous of all wars is a war with savages, though it is apt to be also the most terrible and inhuman. The rude, fierce settler who drives the savage from the land lays all civilized mankind under a debt to him. . . . [I]t is of incalculable importance that America, Australia, and Siberia should pass out of the hands of their red, black, and yellow aboriginal owners, and become the heritage of the dominant world races.

The Winning of the West, 1889

Popular sentiment is just when it selects as popular heroes the men who have led in the struggle against malice domestic or foreign levy. No triumph of peace is quite so great as the supreme triumphs of war. The courage of the soldier, the courage of the statesman who has to meet storms which can be quelled only by soldierly qualities—this stands higher than any quality called out merely in time of peace. It is by no means necessary that we should have war to develop soldierly attributes and soldierly qualities; but if the peace we enjoy is of such kind that it causes their loss, then it is far too dearly purchased, no matter what may be its at-

tendant benefits. It may be that some time in the dim future
of the race the need for war will vanish; but that time is yet
ages distant. As yet no nation can hold its place in the
world, or can do any work really worth doing, unless it
stands ready to guard its rights with an armed hand.

"Washington's Forgotten Maxim," address
before the Naval War College, Newport,
Rhode Island, June 2, 1897

If in the future we have war, it will almost certainly come
because of some action or lack of action, on our part in the
way of refusing to accept responsibilities at the proper time,
or failing to prepare for war when war does not threaten.
An ignoble peace is even worse than an unsuccessful war;
but an unsuccessful war would leave behind it a legacy of
bitter memories which would hurt our national development for a generation to come. It is true that no nation could
actually conquer us, owing to our isolated position; but we
would be seriously harmed, even materially, by disasters
that stopped far short of conquest; and in these matters,
which are far more important than things material, we
could readily be damaged beyond repair. No material loss
can begin to compensate for the loss of national self-respect.

Ibid.

A really great people, proud and high-spirited, would face
all the disasters of war rather than purchase that base prosperity which is bought at the price of national honor.

"Athletics, Scholarship, and Public Service,"
address to Harvard Union, Cambridge,
Massachusetts, February 23, 1907

I abhor war. In common with all other thinking men I am
inexpressibly saddened by the dreadful contest now raging
in Europe. I put peace very high as an agent for bringing

about righteousness. But if I must choose between righteousness and peace, I choose righteousness.
    America and the World War, 1915

Wars between civilized communities are very dreadful, and as nations grow more and more civilized we have every reason, not merely to hope, but to believe that they will grow rarer and rarer. Even with civilized peoples, as was shown by our own experience in 1861, it may be necessary at last to draw the sword than to submit to wrong-doing. But a very marked feature in the world-history of the present century has been the growing infrequency of wars between great civilized nations.
    "Expansion and Peace," in The Strenuous Life, 1900

Booker T. Washington

As to the Booker T. Washington incident, I had no thought whatever of anything save of having a chance of showing some little respect to a man whom I cordially esteem as a good citizen and good American. The outburst of feeling in the South about it is to me literally inexplicable. It does not anger me. As far as I am personally concerned I regard their attacks with the most contemptuous indifference, but I am very melancholy that such feeling should exist in such bitterly aggravated form in any part of our country.
    TR to Lucius Nathan Littauer, October 24, 1901,
    Letters

I am sorry to say that the idiot or vicious Bourbon element of the South is crazy because I have had Booker T. Washington to dine. I shall have him to dine just as often as I please. . . .
    TR to Curtis Guild, October 28, 1901, Letters

In this incident I deserve no particular credit. When I asked Booker T. Washington to dinner I did not devote very much thought to the matter one way or the other. I respect him greatly and believe in the work he has done. I have consulted so much with him it seemed to me that it was natural to ask him to dinner to talk over this work, and the very fact that I felt a moment's qualm on inviting him because of his color made me ashamed of myself and made me hasten to send the invitation. I did not think of its bearing one way or the other, either on my own future or on anything else. As things have turned out, I am very glad that I asked him, for the clamor aroused by the act makes me feel as if the act was necessary.

> *TR to Albion Winegar Tourgee,*
> *November 8, 1901, Letters*

Weasel Words

One of our defects as a nation is a tendency to use what have been called "weasel words." When a weasel sucks eggs the meat is sucked out of the egg. If you use a "weasel word" after another, there is nothing left of the other.

> *Speech at St. Louis, Missouri, May 13, 1916*

Woodrow Wilson

Woodrow Wilson is a perfect trump. I am overjoyed at his election [to president of Princeton University].

> *TR to Cleveland Hoadley Dodge, June 16, 1902,*
> *Letters*

I have long regarded Mr. Wilson as one of the men who had constructive scholarship and administrative ability; and I am very glad from every standpoint that he is to be the new President of Princeton.

> *TR to Grover Cleveland, June 17, 1902, Letters*

I have been assailed because I have criticised Mr. Wilson. I have not said one thing of him that was not absolutely accurate and truthful. . . . I believe he has dragged in the dust what was most sacred in our past, and has jeopardized the most vital hopes of our future . . . he has played a more evil part than Buchanan and Pierce. . . . I criticise him now because he has adroitly and cleverly and with sinister ability appealed to all that is weakest and most unworthy in the American character. . . . He has made our statesmanship a thing of empty elocution. He has covered his fear of standing for the right behind a veil of rhetorical phrases. He has wrapped the true heart of the nation in a spangled shroud of rhetoric. He has kept the eyes of the people dazzled so that they know not what is real and what is false, so that they turn, bewildered, unable to discern the difference between the glitter that veneers evil and the stark realities of courage and honesty, of truth and strength. In the face of the world he has covered this nation's face with shame as with a garment.

> *"The Soul of the Nation," address delivered at*
> *Cooper Union, New York, November 3, 1916;*
> *in Fear God and Take Your Own Part, 1916*

Wisdom

Nine-tenths of wisdom is being wise in time, and if a country lets the time for wise action pass, it may bitterly repent when a generation later it strives under disheartening difficulties to do what could have been done so easily if attempted at the right moment.

> *TR to Edward Grey, November 15, 1913,*
> *Letters*

Women

The pangs of childbirth make all men the debtors of all women.

> *TR to Hamlin Garland, July 19, 1903, Letters*

Working women have the same need to combine for protection that working men have; the ballot is as necessary for one class as for the other; we do not believe that with the two sexes there is identity of function; but we do believe there should be equality of right; and therefore we favor woman suffrage.

*"A Confession of Faith," speech at the
national convention of the Progressive Party,
Chicago, Illinois, August 6, 1912*

Much can be done by law towards putting women on a footing of complete and entire equal rights with man—including the right to vote, the right to hold and use property, and the right to enter any profession she desires on the same terms as the man.

Autobiography, 1913

Women should have free access to every field of labor which they care to enter, and when their work is as valuable as that of a man it should be paid as highly.

Ibid.

Work
We can do a great deal when we undertake, soberly, to do the possible. When we undertake the impossible, we often fail to do anything at all.

*"The Labor Question," speech at Labor Day
picnic, Chicago, Illinois, September 3, 1900*

Your work is hard. Do you suppose I mention that because I pity you? No; not a bit. I don't pity any man who does hard work worth doing. I admire him. I pity the creature who doesn't work, at whichever end of the social scale he may regard himself as being. The law of worthy work well done is the law of successful American life. I believe in play, too—play, and play hard while you play; but don't make the mistake of thinking that that is the main thing. The work is what counts, and if a man does his work well and it is worth doing, then it matters but little in which line that work is done; the man is a good American citizen. If he does his work in slipshod fashion, then no matter what kind of work it is, he is not a good American citizen.

Speech to the Brotherhood of Locomotive
Firemen, Chattanooga, Tennessee,
September 8, 1902

No man is happy if he does not work.

Speech at Topeka, Kansas, May 1, 1903

Remember that one first-class bit of work is better than one thousand pretty good bits of work; that as the years roll on the man or the woman who has been able to make a master-piece with the pen, the brush, the pencil, in any way, has rendered a service to the country such as not all his or her compeers who merely do fairly good second-rate work can ever accomplish.

Address at Leland Stanford, Junior, University,
Palo Alto, California, May 12, 1903

No man needs sympathy because he has to work, because he has a burden to carry. Far and away the best prize that life offers is the chance to work hard at work worth doing; and this is a prize open to every man. . . .

"National Unity versus Class Cleavage,"
Labor Day address at New York State Fair,
Syracuse, New York, September 7, 1903

Nothing in this world is worth having or worth doing unless it means effort, pain, difficulty. I know that your life is hard; I know that your work is hard; and hardest of all for those of you who have the highest trained consciences, and who therefore feel always how much you ought to do. I know your work is hard, and that is why I congratulate you with all my heart. I have never in my life envied a human being who led an easy life; I have envied a great many people who led difficult lives and led them well.

"American Ideals in Education," address before the Iowa State Teachers' Association, at Des Moines, Iowa, November 4, 1910

Part II

THE EXCERPTS

The Duties of American Citizenship

Of course, in one sense, the first essential for a man's being a good citizen is his possession of the home[ly] virtues of which we think when we call a man by the emphatic adjective of manly. No man can be a good citizen who is not a good husband and a good father, who is not honest in his dealings with other men and women, faithful to his friends and fearless in the presence of his foes, who has not got a sound heart, a sound mind, and a sound body; exactly as no amount of attention to civil duties will save a nation if the domestic life is undermined, or there is lack of the rude military virtues which alone can assure a country's position in the world. In a free republic the ideal citizen must be one willing and able to take arms for the defense of the flag, exactly as the ideal citizen must be the father of many healthy children. A race must be strong and vigorous; it must be a race of good fighters and good breeders, else its wisdom will come to naught and its virtue be ineffective; and no sweetness and delicacy, no love for and appreciation of beauty in art or literature, no capacity for building up material prosperity, can possibly atone for the lack of the great virile virtues.

But this is aside from my subject, for what I wish to talk of is the attitude of the American citizen in civic life. It ought to be axiomatic in this country that every man must

Address before the Liberal Club, Buffalo, New York, January 26, 1893; in American Ideals (Works, vol. 13)

devote a reasonable share of his time to doing his duty in the political life of the community. No man has a right to shirk his political duties under whatever plea of pleasure or business; and while such shirking may be pardoned in those of small means, it is entirely unpardonable in those among whom it is most common—in the people whose circumstances give them freedom in the struggle for life. In so far as the community grows to think rightly, it will likewise grow to regard the young man of means who shirks his duty to the State in time of peace as being only one degree worse than the man who thus shirks it in time of war. A great many of our men in business, or of our young men who are bent on enjoying life (as they have a perfect right to do if only they do not sacrifice other things to enjoyment), rather plume themselves upon being good citizens if they even vote; yet voting is the very least of their duties. Nothing worth gaining is ever gained without effort. You can no more have freedom without striving and suffering for it than you can win success as a banker or a lawyer without labor and effort, without self-denial in youth and the display of a ready and alert intelligence in middle age. The people who say that they have not time to attend to politics are simply saying that they are unfit to live in a free community. Their place is under a despotism; or if they are content to do nothing but vote, you can take despotism tempered by an occasional plebescite, like that of the second Napoleon. In one of Lowell's magnificent stanzas about the Civil War he speaks of the fact which his countrymen were then learning, that freedom is not a gift that tarries long in the hands of cowards: nor yet does it tarry long in the hands of the sluggard and the idler, in the hands of the man so much absorbed in the pursuit of pleasure or in the pursuit of gain, or so much wrapped up in his own easy home life as to be unable to take his part in the rough struggle with his fellow men for political supremacy. If freedom is worth having, if the right of self-government is a valuable right, then the one and the other must be retained exactly as our forefathers acquired them, by labor, and especially by labor in organization; that is, in combination with our fellows who have the same interests and the same principles. We should not accept the excuse of the business man who attributed his failure to the fact that his social duties were so pleasant and engrossing that he had no time left for work in his office; nor would we pay much heed to his further statement that he did not like business anyhow because he thought the morals of the business community by no means what they should be, and saw that the great successes were most often won by men of the Jay Gould stamp. It is just the same way with politics. It makes one feel half angry and half amused, and wholly contemptuous, to find men of high business or social standing in the community saying that they really have not got time to go to ward meetings, to organize political clubs, and to take a personal share in all the important details of practical politics; men who further urge against their going the fact that they think the condition of political morality low, and are afraid that they may be required to do what is not right if they go into politics.

The first duty of an American citizen, then, is that he shall work in politics; his second duty is that he shall do that work in a practical manner; and his third is that it shall be done in accord with the highest principles of honor and justice. Of course, it is not possible to define rigidly just the way in which the work shall be made practical. Each man's individual temper and convictions must be taken into account. To a certain extent his work must be done in accordance with his individual beliefs and theories of right and wrong. To a yet greater extent it must be done in combination with others, he yielding or modifying certain of his own theories and beliefs so as to enable him to stand on a common ground with his fellows, who have likewise yielded or modified certain of their theories and beliefs. There is no need of dogmatizing about independence on the one hand or party allegiance on the other. There are occasions when it may be the highest duty of any man to act outside of parties and against the one with which he has himself been hitherto identified; and there may be many more occasions when his highest duty is to sacrifice some of his own cherished opinions for the sake of the success of the party which he on the whole believes to be right. I do not think that the average citizen, at least in one of our great cities, can very well manage to support his own party all the time on every issue, local and otherwise; at any rate if he can do so he has been more fortunately placed than I have been. On the other hand, I am fully convinced that to do the best work people must be organized; and of course an organization is really a party, whether it be a great organization covering the whole nation and numbering its millions of adherents, or an association of citizens in a particular locality, banded together to win a certain specific victory, as, for instance, that of municipal reform. Somebody has said that a racing-yacht, like a good rifle, is a bundle of incompatibilities; that you must get the utmost possible sail power without sacrificing any other quality, and yet that you cannot help sacrificing some other quality if you really do get the utmost sail power; that, in short, you have got to make more or less of a compromise on each in order to acquire the dozen things needful; but, of course, in making this compromise you must be very careful for the sake of something unimportant not to sacrifice any of the great principles of successful naval architecture. Well, it is about so with a man's political work. He has got to preserve his independence on the one hand; and on the other, unless he wishes to be a wholly ineffective crank, he has got to have some sense of party allegiance and party responsibility, and he has got to realize that in any given exigency it may be a matter of duty to sacrifice one quality, or it may be a matter of duty to sacrifice the other.

If it is difficult to lay down any fixed rules for party action in the abstract; it would, of course, be wholly impossible to lay them down for party action in the concrete, with reference to the organization of the present day. I think that we ought to be broad-minded enough to recognize the fact that a good citizen, striving with fearlessness, honesty, and common sense to do his best for the nation, can render service to it in many different ways, and by connection with many different organizations. It is well for a man if he is able conscientiously to feel that his views on the great questions of the day, on such questions as the tariff, finance, immigration, the regulation of the liquor traffic, and others like them, are such as to put him in accord with the bulk of those of his fellow citizens who compose one of the greatest parties: but it is perfectly supposable that he may feel so strongly for or against certain principles held by one party, or certain principles held by the other, that he is unable to give his full adherence to either. In such a case I feel that he has no right to plead this lack of agreement with either party as an excuse for refraining from active political work prior to election. It will, of course, bar him from the primaries of the two leading parties, and preclude him from doing his share in organizing their management; but, unless he is very unfortunate, he can surely find a number of men who are in the same position as himself and who agree with him on some specific piece of political work, and they can turn in practically and effectively long before election to try to do this new piece of work in a practical manner.

One seemingly very necessary caution to utter is, that a man who goes into politics should not expect to reform everything right off, with a jump. I know many excellent young men who, when awakened to the fact that they have neglected their political duties, feel an immediate impulse

to form themselves into an organization which shall forthwith purify politics everywhere, national, State, and city
alike; and I know of a man who having gone round once to
a primary, and having, of course, been unable to accomplish anything in a place where he knew no one and could
not combine with any one, returned saying it was quite useless for a good citizen to try to accomplish anything in such
a manner. To these too hopeful or too easily discouraged
people I always feel like reading Artemus Ward's article
upon the people of his own town who came together in a
meeting to resolve that the two should support the Union
and the Civil War, but were unwilling to take any part in
putting down the rebellion unless they could go as
brigadier-generals. After the battle of Bull Run there were a
good many hundreds of thousands of young men in the
North who felt it to be their duty to enter the Northern
armies; but no one of them who possessed much intelligence
expected to take high place at the outset, or anticipated that
individual action would be of decisive importance in any
given campaign. He went in as private or sergeant, lieu-
tenant or captain, as the case might be, and did his duty in
his company, in his regiment, after a while in his brigade.
When Ball's Bluff and Bull Run succeeded the utter failure
of the Peninsular campaign, when the terrible defeat of
Fredericksburg was followed by the scarcely less disastrous
day at Chancellorsville, he did not announce (if he had any
pluck or manliness about him) that he considered it quite
useless for any self-respecting citizen to enter the Army of
the Potomac, because he really was not of much weight in
its councils, and did not approve of its management; he
simply gritted his teeth and went doggedly on with his
duty, grieving over, but not disheartened at the innumerable shortcomings and follies committed by those who
helped to guide the destinies of the army, recognizing also
the bravery, the patience, intelligence, and resolution with

which other men in high places offset the follies and short-comings, and persevering with equal mind through triumph and defeat, until finally he saw the tide of failure turn at Gettysburg and the full flood of victory come with Appomattox.

I do wish that more of our good citizens would go into politics, and would do it in the same spirit with which their fathers went into the Federal armies. Begin with the little thing, and do not expect to accomplish anything without an effort. Of course, if you go to a primary just once, never having taken the trouble to know any of the other people who go there, you will find yourself wholly out of place; but if you keep on attending and try to form associations with other men whom you meet at the political gatherings, or whom you can persuade to attend them, you will very soon find yourself a weight. In the same way, if a man feels that the politics of his city, for instance, are very corrupt and wants to reform them, it would be an excellent idea for him to begin with his district. If he joins with other people, who think as he does, to form a club where abstract political virtue will be discussed he may do a great deal of good. We need such clubs: but he must also get to know his own ward or his own district, put himself in communication with the decent people in that district, of whom we may rest assured there will be many, willing and able to do something practical for the procurance of better government. Let him set to work to procure a better assemblyman or better alderman before he tries his hand at making a mayor, a governor, or a president. If he begins at the top he may make a brilliant temporary success, but the chances are a thousand to one that he will only be defeated eventually; and in no event will the good he does stand on the same broad and permanent foundation as if he had begun at the bottom. Of course, one or two of his efforts may be failures; but if he has the right stuff in him he will go ahead and do his duty irrespective of whether he meets with success or defeat. It is perfectly right to consider the question of failure while shaping one's efforts to succeed in the struggle for the right; but there should be no consideration of it whatsoever when the question is as to whether one should or should not make a struggle for the right. When once a band of one hundred and fifty or two hundred honest, intelligent men, who mean business and know their business, is found in any district, whether in one of the regular organizations or outside, you can guarantee that the local politicians of that district will begin to treat it with a combination of fear, hatred, and respect, and that its influence will be felt; and that while sometimes men will be elected to office in direct defiance of its wishes, more often the successful candidates will feel that they have to pay some regard to its demands for public decency and honesty.

But in advising you to be practical and to work hard, I must not for one moment be understood as advising you to abandon one iota of your self-respect and devotion to principle. It is a bad sign for the country to see one class of our citizens sneer at practical politicians, and another at Sunday-school politics. No man can do both effective and decent work in public life unless he is a practical politician on the one hand, and a sturdy believer in Sunday-school politics on the other. He must always strive manfully for the best, and yet, like Abraham Lincoln, must often resign himself to accept the best possible. Of course when a man verges on to the higher ground of statesmanship, when he becomes a leader, he must very often consult with others and defer to their opinion, and must be continually settling in his mind how far he can go in just deference to the wishes and prejudices of others while yet adhering to his own moral standards: but I speak not so much of men of this stamp as I do of the ordinary citizen, who wants to do his duty as a member of the commonwealth in its civic life;

and for this man I feel that the one quality which he ought always to hold most essential is that of disinterestedness. If he once begins to feel that he wants office himself, with a willingness to get it at the cost of his convictions, or to keep it when gotten, at the cost of his convictions, his usefulness is gone. Let him make up his mind to do his duty in politics without regard to holding office at all, and let him know that often the men in this country who have done the best work for our public life have not been the men in office. If, on the other hand, he attains public position, let him not strive to plan out for himself a career. I do not think that any man should let himself regard his political career as a means of livelihood, or as his sole occupation in life; for if he does he immediately becomes most seriously handicapped. The moment that he begins to think how such and such an act will affect the voters in his district, or will affect some great political leader who will have an influence over his destiny, he is hampered and his hands are bound. Not only may it be his duty often to disregard the wishes of politicians, but it may be his clear duty at times to disregard the wishes of the people. The voice of the people is not always the voice of God; and when it happens to be the voice of the devil, then it is a man's clear duty to defy its behests. Different political conditions breed different dangers. The demagogue is as unlovely a creature as the courtier, though one is fostered under republican and the other under monarchical institutions. There is every reason why a man should have an honorable ambition to enter public life, and an honorable ambition to stay there when he is in; but he ought to make up his mind that he cares for it only as long as he can stay in it on his own terms, without sacrifice of his own principles; and if he does thus make up his mind he can really accomplish twice as much for the nation, and can reflect a hundredfold greater honor upon himself, in a short term of service, than can the man who grows gray in the

public employment at the cost of sacrificing what he believes to be true and honest. And moreover, when a public
servant has definitely made up his mind that he will pay no
heed to his own future, but will do what he honestly deems
best for the community, without regard to how his actions
may affect his prospects, not only does he become infinitely
more useful as a public servant, but he has a far better time.
He is freed from the harassing care which is inevitably the
portion of him who is trying to shape his sails to catch every
gust of the wind of political favor.

But let me reiterate, that in being virtuous he must not
become ineffective, and that he must not excuse himself for
shirking his duties by any false plea that he cannot do his
duties and retain his self-respect. This is nonsense, he can;
and when he urges such a plea it is a mark of mere laziness
and self-indulgence. And again, he should beware how he
becomes a critic of the actions of others, rather than a doer
of deeds himself; and in so far as he does act as a critic (and
of course the critic has a great and necessary function) he
must beware of indiscriminate censure even more than of
indiscriminate praise. The screaming vulgarity of the foolish spread-eagle orator who is continually yelling defiance
at Europe, praising everything American, good and bad,
and resenting the introduction of any reform because it has
previously been tried successfully abroad, is offensive and
contemptible to the last degree; but after all it is scarcely as
harmful as the peevish, fretful, sneering, and continual
faultfinding of the refined, well-educated man, who is always attacking good and bad alike, who genuinely dis-
trusts America, and in the true spirit of servile colonialism
considers us inferior to the people across the water. It may
be taken for granted that the man who is always sneering at
our public life and our public men is a thoroughly bad citizen, and that what little influence he wields in the community is wielded for evil. The public speaker or the editorial

writer, who teaches men of education that their proper attitude toward American politics should be one of dislike or
indifference, is doing all he can to perpetuate and aggravate
the very evils of which he is ostensibly complaining. Exactly
as it is generally the case that when a man bewails the decadence of our civilization he is himself physically, mentally,
and morally a first-class type of the decadent, so it is usually the case that when a man is perpetually sneering at
American politicians, whether worthy or unworthy, he
himself is a poor citizen and a friend of the very forces of
evil against which he professes to contend. Too often these
men seem to care less for attacking bad men, than for ruin-
ing the characters of good men with whom they disagree on
some public question; and while their influence against the
bad is almost nil, they are sometimes able to weaken the
hands of the good by withdrawing from them support to
which they are entitled; and they thus count in the sum
total of forces that work for evil. They answer to the political prohibitionist, who, in a close contest between a temper-
ance man and a liquor-seller, diverts enough votes from the
former to elect the liquor-seller. Occasionally it is necessary
to beat a pretty good man, who is not quite good enough,
even at the cost of electing a bad one; but it should be thoroughly recognized that this can be necessary only occasionally and indeed, I may say, only in very exceptional cases,
and that as a rule where it is done the effect is thoroughly
unwholesome in every way, and those taking part in it deserve the severest censure from all honest men.

Moreover, the very need of denouncing evil makes it all
the more wicked to weaken the effect of such denunciations
by denouncing also the good. It is the duty of all citizens, irrespective of party, to denounce, and, so far as may be, to
punish crimes against the public on the part of politicians
or officials. But exactly as the public man who commits a
crime against the public is one of the worst of criminals, so,

close on his heels in the race for iniquitous distinction, comes the man who falsely charges the public servant with outrageous wrong-doing; whether it is done with foul-mouthed and foolish directness in the vulgar and violent party organ, or with sarcasm, innuendo, and the half-truths that are worse than lies, in some professed organ of independence. Not only should criticism be honest, but it should be intelligent, in order to be effective. I recently read in a religious paper an article railing at the corruption of our public life, in which it was stated incidentally that the lobby was recognized as all-powerful in Washington. This is untrue. There was a day when the lobby was very important at Washington, but its influence in Congress is now very small indeed; and from a pretty intimate acquaintance with several Congresses I am entirely satisfied that there is among the members a very small proportion indeed who are corruptible, in the sense that they will let their action be influenced by money or its equivalent. Congressmen are very often demagogues; they are very often blind partisans; they are often exceedingly short-sighted, narrow-minded, and bigoted; but they are not usually corrupt; and to accuse a narrow-minded demagogue of corruption when he is perfectly honest, is merely to set him more firmly in his evil course and to help him with his constituents, who recognize that the charge is entirely unjust, and in repelling it lose sight of the man's real shortcomings. I have known more than one State legislature, more than one board of aldermen against which the charge of corruption could perfectly legitimately be brought, but it cannot be brought against Congress. Moreover these sweeping charges really do very little good. When I was in the New York legislature, one of the things that I used to mind most was the fact that at the close of every session the papers that affect morality invariably said that that particular legislature was the worst legislature since the days of Tweed. The statement was not true as a rule; and, in any event, to lump all the members, good and bad, in sweeping condemnation simply hurt the good and helped the bad. Criticism should be fearless, but I again reiterate that it should be honest and should be discriminating. When it is sweeping and unintelligent, and directed against good and bad alike, or against the good and bad qualities of any man alike, it is very harmful. It tends steadily to deteriorate the character of our public men; and it tends to produce a very unwholesome spirit among young men of education, and especially among the young men in our colleges.

Against nothing is fearless and specific criticism more urgently needed than against the "spoils system," which is the degradation of American politics. And nothing is more effective in thwarting the purposes of the spoilsmen than the civil service reform. To be sure, practical politicians sneer at it. One of them even went so far as to say that civil-service reform is asking a man irrelevant questions. What more irrelevant question could there be than that of the practical politician who asks the aspirant for his political favor—"Whom did you vote for in the last election?" There is certainly nothing more interesting, from a humorous point of view, than the heads of departments urging changes to be made in their underlings, "on the score of increased efficiency" they say; when as the result of such a change the old incumbent often spends six months teaching the new incumbent how to do the work almost as well as he did himself! Occasionally the civil-service reform has been abused, but not often. Certainly the reform is needed when you contemplate the spectacle of a New York City treasurer who acknowledges his annual fees to be eighty-five thousand dollars, and who pays a deputy one thousand five hundred dollars to do his work—when you note the corruptions in the New York legislature, where one man says he has a horror of the Constitution because it prevents active benevolence, and another says that you should never allow the Constitution to come between friends! All these corruptions and vices are what every good American citizen must fight against.

Finally, the man who wishes to do his duty as a citizen in our country must be imbued through and through with the spirit of Americanism. I am not saying this as a matter of spread-eagle rhetoric: I am saying it quite soberly as a piece of matter-of-fact, common-sense advice, derived from my own experience of others. Of course, the question of Americanism has several sides. If a man is an educated man, he must show his Americanism by not getting misled into following out and trying to apply all the theories of the political thinkers of other countries, such as Germany and France, to our own entirely different conditions. He must not get a fad, for instance, about responsible government; and above all things he must not, merely because he is intelligent, or a college professor well read in political literature, try to discuss our institutions when he has had no practical knowledge of how they are worked. Again, if he is a wealthy man, a man of means and standing, he must really feel, not merely affect to feel, that no social differences obtain save such as a man can in some way himself make by his own actions. People sometimes ask me if there is not a prejudice against a man of wealth and education in ward politics. I do not think there is, unless the man in turn shows that he regards the facts of his having wealth and education as giving him a claim to superiority aside from the merit he is able to prove himself to have in actual service. Of course, if he feels that he ought to have a little better treatment than a carpenter, a plumber, or a butcher, who happens to stand beside him, he is going to be thrown out of the race very quickly, and probably quite roughly; and if he starts in to patronize and elaborately condescend to these men he will find that they resent this attitude even more. Do not let him think about the matter at all. Let him go into the political contest with no more thought of such matters than a college boy gives to the social standing of the members of his own and rival teams in a hotly contested football-match. As soon as he begins to take an interest in politics (and he will speedily not only get interested for the sake of politics, but also take a good healthy interest in playing the game itself—an interest which is perfectly normal and praiseworthy, and to which only a prig would object), he will begin to work up the organization in the way that will be most effective, and he won't care a rap about who is put to work with him, save in so far as he is a good fellow and an efficient worker. There was one time that a number of men who think as we do here to-night (one of the number being myself) got hold of one of the assembly districts of New York, and ran it in really an ideal way, better than any other assembly district has ever been run before or since by either party. We did it by hard work and good organization; by working practically, and yet by being honest and square in motive and method: especially did we do it by all turning in as straight-out Americans without any regard to distinctions of race origin. Among the many men who did a great deal in organizing our victories was the son of a Presbyterian clergyman, the nephew of a Hebrew rabbi, and two well-known Catholic gentlemen. We also had a Columbia College professor (the stroke-oar of a university crew), a noted retail butcher, the editor of a local German paper, various brokers, bankers, lawyers, bricklayers, and a stone-mason who was particularly useful to us, although on questions of theoretic rather than applied politics he had a decidedly socialistic turn of mind.

Again, questions of race origin, like questions of creed, must not be considered: we wish to do good work, and we are all Americans, pure and simple. In the New York legislature, when it fell to my lot to choose a committee—which

I always esteemed my most important duty at Albany—no less than three out of the four men I chose were of Irish birth or parentage; and three abler and more fearless and disinterested men never sat in a legislative body; while among my especial political and personal friends in that body was a gentleman from the southern tier of counties, who was, I incidentally found out, a German by birth, but who was just as straight United States as if his ancestors had come over here in the *Mayflower* or in Henry Hudson's yacht. Of course, none of these men of Irish or German birth would have been worth their salt had they continued to act after coming here as Irishmen or Germans, or as anything but plain straight-out Americans. We have not any room here for a divided allegiance. A man has got to be an American and nothing else; and he has no business to be mixing us up with questions of foreign politics, British or Irish, German or French, and no business to try to perpetuate their language and customs in the land of complete religious toleration and equality. If, however, he does become honestly and in good faith an American, then he is entitled to stand precisely as all other Americans stand, and it is the height of un-Americanism to discriminate against him in any way because of creed or birthplace. No spirit can be more thoroughly alien to American institutions than the spirit of the Know-nothings.

In facing the future and in striving, each according to the measure of his individual capacity, to work out the salvation of our land, we should be neither timid pessimists nor foolish optimists. We should recognize the dangers that exist and that threaten us: we should neither overestimate them nor shrink from them, but steadily fronting them should set to work to overcome and beat them down. Grave perils are yet to be encountered in the stormy course of the Republic—perils from political corruption, perils from individual laziness, indolence and timidity, perils springing from the greed of the unscrupulous rich, and from the anarchic violence of the thriftless and turbulent poor. There is every reason why we should recognize them, but there is no reason why we should fear them or doubt our capacity to overcome them, if only each will, according to the measure of his ability, do his full duty, and endeavor so to live as to deserve the high praise of being called a good American citizen.

Washington's Forgotten Maxim

A century has passed since Washington wrote "To be prepared for war is the most effectual means to promote peace." We pay to this maxim the lip loyalty we so often pay to Washington's words; but it has never sunk deep into our hearts. Indeed of late years many persons have refused it even the poor tribute of lip loyalty, and prate about the iniquity of war as if somehow that was a justification for refusing to take the steps which can alone in the long run prevent war or avert the dreadful disasters it brings in its train. The truth of the maxim is so obvious to every man of really far-sighted patriotism that its mere statement seems trite and useless; and it is not over-creditable to either our intelligence or our love of country that there should be, as there is, need to dwell upon and amplify such a truism.

In this country there is not the slightest danger of an overdevelopment of warlike spirit, and there never has been any such danger. In all our history there has never been a time when preparedness for war was any menace to peace. On the contrary, again and again we have owed peace to the fact that we were prepared for war; and in the only contest which we have had with a European power since the Revolution, the war of 1812, the struggle and all its

Address before the Naval War College, Newport, Rhode Island, June 1897; in American Ideals (Works, vol. 13)

attendant disasters were due solely to the fact that we were not prepared to face, and were not ready instantly to resent, an attack upon our honor and interest; while the glorious triumphs at sea which redeemed that war were due to the few preparations which we had actually made. We are a great peaceful nation; a nation of merchants and manufacturers, of farmers and mechanics; a nation of workingmen, who labor incessantly with head or hand. It is idle to talk of such a nation ever being led into a course of wanton aggression or conflict with military powers by the possession of a sufficient navy.

The danger is of precisely the opposite character. If we forget that in the last resort we can only secure peace by being ready and willing to fight for it, we may some day have bitter cause to realize that a rich nation which is slothful, timid, or unwieldy is an easy prey for any people which still retains those most valuable of all qualities, the soldierly virtues. We but keep to the traditions of Washington, to the traditions of all the great Americans who struggled for the real greatness of America, when we strive to build up those fighting qualities for the lack of which in a nation, as in an individual, no refinement, no culture, no wealth, no material prosperity, can atone.

Preparation for war is the surest guaranty for peace. Arbitration is an excellent thing, but ultimately those who wish to see this country at peace with foreign nations will be wise if they place reliance upon a first-class fleet of first-class battleships rather than on any arbitration treaty which the wit of man can devise. Nelson said that the British fleet was the best negotiator in Europe, and there was much truth in the saying. Moreover, while we are sincere and earnest in our advocacy of peace, we must not forget that an ignoble peace is worse than any war. We should engrave in our legislative halls those splendid lines of Lowell:

"Come, Peace! not like a mourner bowed
For honor lost and dear ones wasted,
But proud, to meet a people proud,
With eyes that tell of triumph tasted!"

Peace is a goddess only when she comes with sword girt on thigh. The ship of state can be steered safely only when it is always possible to bring her against any foe with "her leashed thunders gathering for the leap." A really great people, proud and high-spirited, would face all the disasters of war rather than purchase that base prosperity which is bought at the price of national honor. All the great masterful races have been fighting races, and the minute that a race loses the hard fighting virtues, then, no matter what else it may retain, no matter how skilled in commerce and finance, in science or art, it has lost its proud right to stand as the equal of the best. Cowardice in a race, as in an individual, is the unpardonable sin, and a wilful failure to prepare for danger may in its effects be as bad as cowardice. The timid man who cannot fight, and the selfish, shortsighted, or foolish man who will not take the steps that will enable him to fight, stand on almost the same plane.

It is not only true that a peace may be so ignoble and degrading as to be worse than any war; it is also true that it may be fraught with more bloodshed than most wars. Of this there has been melancholy proof during the last two years. Thanks largely to the very unhealthy influence of the men whose business it is to speculate in the money market, and who approach every subject from the financial standpoint, purely; and thanks quite as much to the cold-blooded brutality and calculating timidity of many European rulers and statesmen, the peace of Europe has been preserved, while the Turk has been allowed to butcher the Armenians with hideous and unmentionable barbarity, and has actually been helped to keep Crete in slavery. War has been

averted at the cost of bloodshed and infinitely more suffering and degradation to wretched women and children than
have occurred in any European struggle, since the days of
Waterloo. No war of recent years, no matter how wanton,
has been so productive of horrible misery as the peace
which the powers have maintained during the continuance
of the Armenian butcheries. The men who would preach
this peace, and indeed the men who have preached universal peace in terms that have prepared the way for such a
peace as this, have inflicted a wrong on humanity greater
than could be inflicted by the most reckless and war-loving
despot. Better a thousand times err on the side of over-
readiness to fight, than to err on the side of tame submission to injury, or cold-blooded indifference to the misery of
the oppressed.

Popular sentiment is just when it selects as popular heroes the men who have led in the struggle against malice
domestic or foreign levy. No triumph of peace is quite so
great as the supreme triumphs of war. The courage of the
soldier, the courage of the statesman who has to meet
storms which can be quelled only by soldierly qualities—
this stands higher than any quality called out merely in
time of peace. It is by no means necessary that we should
have war to develop soldierly attributes and soldierly qualities; but if the peace we enjoy is of such kind that it causes
their loss, then it is far too dearly purchased, no matter
what may be its attendant benefits. It may be that some
time in the dim future of the race the need for war will vanish; but that time is yet ages distant. As yet no nation can
hold its place in the world, or can do any work really worth
doing, unless it stands ready to guard its rights with an
armed hand. That orderly liberty which is both the foundation and the capstone of our civilization can be gained and
kept only by men who are willing to fight for an ideal; who
hold high the love of honor, love of faith, love of flag, and

love of country. It is true that no nation can be really great unless it is great in peace; in industry, integrity, honesty. Skilled intelligence in civic affairs and industrial enterprises alike; the special ability of the artist, the man of letters, the man of science, and the man of business; the rigid determination to wrong no man, and to stand for righteousness— all these are necessary in a great nation. But it is also necessary that the nation should have physical no less than moral courage; the capacity to do and dare and die at need, and that grim and steadfast resolution which alone will carry a great people through a great peril. The occasion may come at any instant when

> " 'Tis man's perdition to be safe
> When for the truth he ought to die."

All great nations have shown these qualities. The Dutch held but a little corner of Europe. Their industry, thrift, and enterprise in the pursuits of peace and their cultivation of the arts helped to render them great; but these qualities would have been barren had they not been backed by those sterner qualities which rendered them able to wrest their freedom from the cruel strength of Spain, and to guard it against the banded might of England and of France. The merchants and the artists of Holland did much for her; but even more was done by the famished burghers who fought to the death on the walls of Haarlem and Leyden, and the great admirals who led their fleets to victory on the broad and narrow seas.

England's history is rich in splendid names and splendid deeds. Her literature is even greater than that of Greece. In commerce she has stood in the modern world as more than ever Carthage was when civilization clustered in a fringe around the Mediterranean. But she has risen far higher than ever Greece or Carthage rose, because she possesses also the great, masterful qualities which were possessed by the

Romans who overthrew them both. England has been fertile in soldiers and administrators; in men who triumphed by sea and by land; in adventurers and explorers who won for her the world's waste spaces; and it is because of this that the English-speaking race now shares with the Slav the fate of the coming years.

We of the United States have passed most of our few years of national life in peace. We honor the architects of our wonderful material prosperity; we appreciate the necessity of thrift, energy, and business enterprise, and we know that even these are of no avail without the civic and social virtues. But we feel, after all, that the men who have dared greatly in war, or the work which is akin to war, are those who deserve best of the country. The men of Bunker Hill and Trenton, Saratoga and Yorktown, the men of New Orleans and Mobile Bay, Gettysburg and Appomattox are those to whom we owe most. None of our heroes of peace, save a few great constructive statesmen, can rank with our heroes of war. The Americans who stand highest on the list of the world's worthies are Washington, who fought to found the country which he afterward governed, and Lincoln, who saved it through the blood of the best and bravest in the land; Washington, the soldier and statesman, the man of cool head, dauntless heart, and iron will, the greatest of good men and the best of great men; and Lincoln, sad, patient, kindly Lincoln, who for four years toiled and suffered for the people, and when his work was done laid down his life that the flag which had been rent in sunder might once more be made whole and without a seam.

It is on men such as these, and not on the advocates of peace at any price, or upon those so short-sighted that they refuse to take into account the possibility of war, that we must rely in every crisis which deeply touches the true greatness and true honor of the Republic. The United States has never once in the course of its history suffered harm because of preparation for war, or because of entering into war. But we have suffered incalculable harm, again and again, from a foolish failure to prepare for war or from reluctance to fight when to fight was proper. The men who today protest against a navy, and protest also against every movement to carry out the traditional policy of the country in foreign affairs, and to uphold the honor of the flag, are themselves but following in the course of those who protested against the acquisition of the great West, and who failed to make proper preparations for the war of 1812, or refused to support it after it had been made. They are own brothers to the men whose short-sightedness and supine indifference prevented any reorganization of the *personnel* of the Navy during the middle of the century, so that we entered upon the Civil War with captains seventy years old. They are close kin to the men who, when the Southern States seceded, wished to let the Union be disrupted in peace rather than restored through the grim agony of armed conflict.

I do not believe that any considerable number of our citizens are stamped with this timid lack of patriotism. There are some *doctrinaires* whose eyes are so firmly fixed on the golden vision of universal peace that they cannot see the grim facts of real life until they stumble over them, to their own hurt, and, what is much worse, to the possible undoing of their fellows. There are some educated men in whom education merely serves to soften the fibre and to eliminate the higher, sterner qualities which tell for national greatness; and these men prate about love for mankind, or for another country, as being in some hidden way a substitute for love of their own country. What is of more weight, there are not a few men of means who have made the till their fatherland, and who are always read to balance a temporary interruption of moneymaking, or a temporary financial and com-

mercial disaster, against the self-sacrifice necessary in upholding the honor of the nation and the glory of the flag.

But after all these people, though often noisy, form but a
small minority of the whole. They would be swept like
chaff before the gust of popular fury which would surely
come if ever the nation really saw and felt a danger or an insult. The real trouble is that in such a case this gust of popular fury would come too late. Unreadiness for war is merely
rendered more disastrous by readiness to bluster; to talk defiance and advocate a vigorous policy in words, while refusing to back up these words by deeds, is cause for
humiliation. It has always been true, and in this age it is
more than ever true, that it is too late to prepare for war
when the time for peace has passed. The short-sightedness
of many people, the good-humored indifference to facts of
others, the sheer ignorance of a vast number, and the selfish
reluctance to insure against future danger by present sacrifice among yet others—these are the chief obstacles to
building up a proper navy and carrying out a proper foreign policy.

The men who opposed the war of 1812, and preferred to
have the nation humiliated by unresented insult from a
foreign power rather than see her suffer the losses of an
honorable conflict, occupied a position little short of contemptible; but it was not much worse than that of the men
who brought on the war and yet deliberately refused to
make the preparations necessary to carry it to a successful
conclusion. The visionary schemes for defending the country by gunboats, instead of by a fleet of seagoing battle-
ships; the refusal to increase the Navy to a proper size; the
determination to place reliance upon militia instead of
upon regularly trained troops; and the disasters which followed upon each and every one of these determinations
should be studied in every school-book in the land so as to
enforce in the minds of all our citizens the truth of Washing-

ton's adage, that in time of peace it is necessary to prepare for war.

All this applied in 1812 but it applies with tenfold greater force now. Then, as now, it was the navy upon which the country had to depend in the event of war with a foreign power; and then, as now, one of the chief tasks of a wise and far-seeing statesmanship should have been the upbuilding of a formidable fighting navy. In 1812 untold evils followed from the failure to provide such a fighting navy; for the splendid feats of our few cruisers merely showed what could have been done if we had had a great fleet of battle-ships. But ships, guns, and men were much more easily provided in time of emergency at the beginning of this century than at the end. It takes months to build guns and ships now, where it then took days, or at the most, weeks; and it takes far longer now to train men to the management of the vast and complicated engines with which war is waged. Therefore preparation is much more difficult, and requires a much longer time; and yet wars are so much quicker, they last so comparatively short a period, and can be begun so instantaneously that there is very much less time than formerly in which to make preparations.

No battle-ship can be built inside of two years under no matter what stress of circumstances, for we have not in this country the plant to enable us to work faster. Cruisers would take almost as long. Even torpedo boats, the smallest of all, could not be put in first-class form under ninety days. Guns available for use against a hostile invader would require two or three months; and in the case of the larger guns, the only one really available for the actual shock of battle, could not be made under eight months. Rifles and military munitions of every kind would require a corresponding length of time for preparation; in most cases we should have to build, not merely the weapons we need, but the plant with which to make them in any large quantity.

Even if the enemy did not interfere with our efforts, which they undoubtedly would, it would, therefore, take from three to six months after the outbreak of a war, for which we were unprepared, before we could in the slightest degree remedy our unreadiness. During this six months it would be impossible to overestimate the damage that could be done by a resolute and powerful antagonist. Even at the end of that time we would only be beginning to prepare to parry his attack, for it would be two years before we could attempt to return it. Since the change in military conditions in modern times there has never been an instance in which a war between two nations has lasted more than about two years. In most recent wars the operations of the first ninety days have decided the result of the conflict. All that followed has been a mere vain effort to strive against the stars in their courses by doing at the twelfth hour what it was useless to do after the eleventh.

We must therefore make up our minds once for all to the fact that it is too late to make ready for war when the fight has once begun. The preparation must come before that. In the case of the Civil War none of these conditions applied. In 1861 we had a good fleet, and the Southern Confederacy had not a ship. We were able to blockade the Southern ports at once, and we could improvise engines of war more than sufficient to put against those of any enemy who also had to improvise them, and who labored under even more serious disadvantages. The *Monitor* was got ready in the nick of time to meet the *Merrimac,* because the Confederates had to plan and build the latter while we were planning and building the former; but if ever we have to go to war with a modern military power we shall find its Merrimacs already built, and it will then be altogether too late to try to build Monitors to meet them.

If this point needs any emphasis surely the history of the war of 1812 applies to it. For twelve years before that war broke out even the blindest could see that we were almost certain to be drawn into hostilities with one or the other of the pair of combatants whose battle royal ended at Waterloo. Yet we made not the slightest preparation for war. The authorities at Washington contented themselves with trying to build a flotilla of gunboats which could defend our own harbors without making it necessary to take the offensive ourselves. We already possessed a dozen first-class cruisers, but not a battle-ship of any kind. With almost incredible folly the very Congress that declared war voted down the bill to increase the Navy by twenty battle-ships; though it was probably too late then, anyhow, for even under the simpler conditions of that day such a fleet could not have been built and put into first-class order in less than a couple of years. Bitterly did the nation pay for its want of foresight and forethought. Our cruisers won a number of striking victories, heartening and giving hope to the nation in the face of disaster; but they were powerless to do material harm to the gigantic naval strength of Great Britain. Efforts were made to increase our little Navy, but in the face of a hostile enemy already possessing command of the seas this was impossible. Two or three small cruisers were built; but practically almost all the fighting on the ocean was done by the handful of frigates and sloops which we possessed when the war broke out. Not a battle-ship was able to put to sea until after peace was restored. Meanwhile our coast was blockaded from one end to the other and was harried at will by the hostile squadrons. Our capital city was burned, and the ceaseless pressure of the blockade produced such suffering and irritation as nearly to bring about a civil war among ourselves. If in the first decade of the present century the American people and their rulers had possessed the wisdom to provide an efficient fleet of powerful battle-ships there would probably have been no war of 1812; and even if war had come, the immense loss to, and destruction of, trade and commerce by the blockade would have been prevented. Merely from the monetary standpoint the saving would have been incalculable; and yet this would have been the smallest part of the gain.

It can therefore be taken for granted that there must be adequate preparation for conflict, if conflict is not to mean disaster. Furthermore, this preparation must take the shape of an efficient fighting navy. We have no foe able to conquer or overrun our territory. Our small army should always be kept in first-class condition, and every attention should be paid to the National Guard; but neither on the North nor on the South have we neighbors capable of menacing us with invasion or long resisting a serious effort on our part to invade them. The enemies we may have to face will come from over sea; they may come from Europe, or they may come from Asia. Events move fast in the West; but this generation has been forced to see that they move even faster in the oldest East. Our interests are as great in the Pacific as in the Atlantic, in the Hawaiian Islands as in the West Indies. Merely for the protection of our own shores we need a great navy; and what is more, we need it to protect our interests in the islands from which it is possible to command our shores and to protect our commerce on the high seas.

In building this navy, we must remember two things: First, that our ships and guns should be the very best of their kind; and second, that no matter how good they are, they will be useless unless the man in the conning tower and the man behind the guns are also the best of their kind. It is merely folly to send men to perish because they have arms with which they cannot win. With poor ships, were an Admiral Nelson and Farragut rolled in one, he might be beaten by any first-class fleet; and he surely would be beaten if his opponents were in any degree his equals in skill and courage; but without this skill and courage no perfection of material can avail, and with them very grave short-comings in equipment may be overcome. The men who command our ships must have as perfect weapons ready to their hands as can be found in the civilized world, and they must be trained to the highest point in using them. They must have skill in handling the ships, skill in tactics, skill in strategy, for ignorant courage cannot avail; but without courage neither will skill avail. They must have in them the dogged ability to bear punishment, the power and desire to inflict it, the daring, the resolution, the willingness to take risks and incur responsibility which have been possessed by the great captains of all ages, and without which no man can ever hope to stand in the front rank of fighting men.

Tame submission to foreign aggression of any kind is a mean and unworthy thing; but it is even meaner and more unworthy to bluster first, and then either submit or else refuse to make those preparations which can alone obviate the necessity for submission. I believe with all my heart in the Monroe Doctrine, and, I believe also that the great mass of the American people are loyal to it; but it is worse than idle to announce our adherence to this doctrine and yet to decline to take measures to show that ours is not mere lip loyalty. We had far better submit to interference by foreign powers with the affairs of this continent than to announce that we will not tolerate such interference, and yet refuse to make ready the means by which alone we can prevent it. In public as in private life, a bold front tends to insure peace and not strife. If we possess a formidable navy, small is the chance indeed that we shall ever be dragged into a war to uphold the Monroe Doctrine. If we do not possess such a navy, war may be forced on us at any time.

It is certain, then, that we need a first-class navy. It is equally certain that this should not be merely a navy for defense. Our chief harbors should, of course, be fortified and put in condition to resist the attack of an enemy's fleet; and one of our prime needs is an ample force of torpedo boats to use primarily for coast defense. But in war the mere defensive never plays, and can never result in anything but disaster. It is not enough to parry a blow. The surest way to prevent its repetition is to return it. No master of the prize ring ever fought his way to supremacy by mere dexterity in avoiding punishment. He had to win by inflicting punishment. If the enemy is given the choice of time and place to attack, sooner or later he will do irreparable damage, and if he is at any point beaten back, why, after all, it is merely a repulse, and there are no means of following it up and making it a rout. We cannot rely upon coast protection alone. Forts and heavy land guns and torpedo boats are indispensable, and the last, on occasion, may be used for offensive purposes also. But in the present state of naval and military knowledge we must rely mainly, as all great nations always have relied, on the battle-ship, the fighting ship of the line. Gunboats and light cruisers serve an excellent purpose, and we could not do without them. In time of peace they are the police of the seas; in time of war they would do some harrying of commerce, and a great deal of scouting and skirmishing; but our main reliance must be on the great armored battle-ships with their heavy guns and shot-proof vitals. In the last resort we most trust to the ships whose business it is to fight and not to run, and who can themselves go to sea and strike at the enemy when they choose, instead of waiting peacefully to receive his blow when and where he deems it best to deliver it. If in the event of war our fleet of battle-ships can destroy the hostile fleet, then our coasts are safe from the menace of serious attack; even a fight that ruined our fleet would probably so shatter the hostile fleet as to do away with all chance of invasion; but if we have no fleet wherewith to meet the enemy on the high seas, or to anticipate his stroke by our own, then every city within reach of the tides must spend men and money in preparation for an attack that may not come, but which would cause crushing and irredeemable disaster if it did come.

Still more is it necessary to have a fleet of great battle-ships if we intend to live up to the Monroe Doctrine, and to insist upon its observance in the two Americas and the islands on either side of them. If a foreign power, whether in Europe or Asia, should determine to assert its position in those lands wherein we feel that our influence should be supreme, there is but one way in which we can effectively interfere. Diplomacy is utterly useless where there is no force behind it; the diplomat is the servant, not the master, of the soldier. The prosperity of peace, commercial and materials prosperity, gives no weight whatever when the clash of arms comes. Even great naked strength is useless if there is no immediate means through which that strength can manifest itself. If we mean to protect the people of the lands who look to us for protection from tyranny and aggression; if we mean to uphold our interests in the teeth of the formidable Old World powers, we can only do it by being ready at any time, if the provocation is sufficient, to meet them on the seas, where the battle for supremacy must be fought. Unless we are prepared so to meet them, let us abandon all talk of devotion to the Monroe Doctrine or to the honor of the American name.

This nation cannot stand still if it is to retain its self-respect, and to keep undimmed the honorable traditions inherited from the men who with the sword founded it and by the sword preserved it. We ask that the work of upbuilding the navy, and of putting the United States where it should be put among maritime powers, go forward without a break. We ask this not in the interest of war, but in the interest of peace. No nation should ever wage war wantonly, but no nation should ever avoid it at the cost of the loss of national honor. A nation should never fight unless forced to; but it should always be ready to fight. The mere fact that it is ready will generally spare it the necessity of fighting. If this country now had a fleet of twenty battle-ships their existence would make it all the more likely that we should not have war. It is very important that we should, as a race, keep the virile fighting qualities and should be ready to use them at need; but it is not at all important to use them unless there is need. One of the surest ways to attain these qualities is to keep our navy in first-class trim. There never is, and never has been, on our part a desire to use a weapon because of its being well-tempered. There is not the least danger that the possession of a good navy will render this country overbearing toward its neighbors. The direct contrary is the truth.

An unmanly desire to avoid a quarrel is often the surest way to precipitate one; and utter unreadiness to fight is even surer. If at the time of our trouble with Chili, six years ago, we had not already possessed the nucleus of the new navy we should almost certainly have been forced into fighting, and even as it was trouble was only averted because of the resolute stand then taken by the President and by the officers of the navy who were on the spot. If at that time the Chilians had been able to get ready the battle-ship which was building for them, a war would almost certainly have followed, for we had no battle-ship to put against it.

If in the future we have war, it will almost certainly come because of some action, or lack of action, on our part in the way of refusing to accept responsibilities at the proper time, or failing to prepare for war when war does not threaten. An ignoble peace is even worse than an unsuccessful war; but an unsuccessful war would leave behind it a legacy of bitter memories which would hurt our national development for a generation to come. It is true that no nation could actually conquer us, owing to our isolated position; but we would be seriously harmed, even materially, by disasters that stopped far short of conquest; and in these matters, which are far more important than things material, we could readily be damaged beyond repair. No material loss can begin to compensate for the loss of national self-respect. The damage to our commercial interests by the destruction of one of our coast cities would be as nothing compared to the humiliation which would be felt by every American worthy of the name if we had to submit to such an injury without amply avenging it. It has been finely said that "a gentleman is one who is willing to lay down his life for little things"; that is for those things which seem little to the man who cares only whether shares rise or fall in value, and to the timid *doctrinaire* who preaches timid peace from his cloistered study.

Much of that which is best and highest in national character is made up of glorious memories and traditions. The fight well fought, the life honorably lived, the death bravely met—those count for more in building a high and fine type of temper in a nation than any possible success in the stock market, than any possible prosperity in commerce or manufactures. A rich banker may be a valuable and useful citizen, but not a thousand rich bankers can leave to the country such a heritage as Farragut left, when, lashed in the rigging of the *Hartford*, he forged past the forts and over the unseen death below, to try his wooden stem against the ironclad hull of the great Confederate ram. The people of some given section of our country may be better off because a shrewd and wealthy man has built up therein a great manufacturing business, or has extended a line of railroad past its doors; but the whole nation is better, the whole nation is braver, because Cushing pushed his little torpedo-boat through the darkness to sink beside the sinking *Albemarle*.

Every feat of heroism makes us forever indebted to the man who performed it. All daring and courage, all iron endurance of misfortune, all devotion to the ideal of honor and the glory of the flag, make for a fine and nobler type of manhood. It is not only those who do and dare and endure that are benefited; but also the countless thousands who are not themselves called upon to face the peril, to show the strength or to win the reward. All of us lift our heads higher because those of our countrymen whose trade it is to meet danger have met it well and bravely. All of us are poorer for every base or ignoble deed done by an American, for every instance of selfishness or weakness or folly on the part of the people as a whole. We are all worse off when any of us fails at any point in his duty toward the State in time of peace, or his duty toward the State in time of war. If ever we had to meet defeat at the hands of a foreign foe, or had to submit tamely to wrong or insult, every man among us worthy of the name of American would feel dishonored and debased. On the other hand, the memory of every triumph won by Americans, by just so much helps to make each American nobler and better. Every man among us is more fit to meet the duties and responsibilities of citizenship because of the perils over which, in the past, the nation has triumphed; because of the blood and sweat and tears, the labor and the anguish, through which, in the days that have gone, our forefathers moved on to triumph. There are higher things in this life than the soft and easy enjoyment of material comfort. It is through strife, or the readiness for strife, that a nation must win greatness. We ask for a great navy, partly because we think that the possession of such a navy is the surest guaranty of peace, and partly because we feel that no national life is worth having if the nation is not willing, when the need shall arise, to stake everything on the supreme arbitrament of war, and to pour out its blood, its treasure, and its tears like water, rather than submit to the loss of honor and renown.

In closing, let me repeat that we ask for a great navy, we ask for an armament fit for the nation's needs, not primarily to fight, but to avert fighting. Preparedness deters the foe, and maintains right by the show of ready might without the use of violence. Peace, like freedom, is not a gift that tarries long in the hands of cowards, or of those too feeble or too-short-sighted to deserve it; and we ask to be given the means to insure that honorable peace which alone is worth having.

The Control of Corporations

We are passing through a period of great commercial prosperity, and such a period is as sure as adversity itself to bring mutterings of discontent. At a time when most men prosper somewhat some men always prosper greatly; and it is as true now as when the tower of Siloam fell upon all alike, that good fortune does not come solely to the just, nor bad fortune solely to the unjust. When the weather is good for crops it is good for weeds. Moreover, not only do the wicked flourish when the times are such that most men flourish, but, what is worse, the spirit of envy and jealousy springs up in the breasts of those who, though they may be doing fairly well themselves, see others no more deserving who do better.

Wise laws and fearless and upright administration of the laws can give the opportunity for such prosperity as we see about us. But that is all that they can do. When the conditions have been created which make prosperity possible, then each individual man must achieve it for himself by his own energy and thrift and business intelligence. If when people wax fat they kick, as they have kicked since the days of Jeshurun, they will speedily destroy their own prosperity. If they go into wild speculation and lose their heads

Address at Providence, Rhode Island, August 23, 1902; in American Problems (Works, vol. 16)

they have lost that which no laws can supply. If in a spirit of sullen envy they insist upon pulling down those who have profited most in the years of fatness, they will bury themselves in the crash of the common disaster. It is difficult to make our material condition better by the best laws, but it is easy enough to ruin it by bad laws.

The upshot of all this is that it is peculiarly incumbent upon us in a time of such material well-being, both collectively as a nation and individually as citizens, to show, each on his own account, that we possess the qualities of prudence, self-knowledge, and self-restraint. In our government we need above all things stability, fixity of economic policy; while remembering that this fixity must not be fossilization, that there must not be inability to shift our laws so as to meet our shifting national needs. There are real and great evils in our social and economic life, and these evils stand out in all their ugly baldness in time of prosperity; for the wicked who prosper are never a pleasant sight. There is every need of striving in all possible ways, individually and collectively, by combinations among ourselves and through the recognized governmental agencies, to cut out those evils. All I ask is to be sure that we do not use the knife with an ignorant zeal which would make it more dangerous to the patient than to the disease.

One of the features of the tremendous industrial development of the last generation has been the very great increase in private, and especially in corporate, fortunes. We may like this or not, just as we choose, but it is a fact nevertheless; and as far as we can see it is an inevitable result of the working of the various causes, prominent among them steam and electricity. Urban population has grown in this country, as in all civilized countries, much faster than the population as a whole during the last century. If it were not for that Rhode Island could not to-day be the State she is. Rhode Island has flourished as she has flourished because of the conditions which have brought about the great increase in urban life. There is evil in these conditions, but you can't destroy it unless you destroy the civilization they have brought about. Where men are gathered together in great masses it inevitably results that they must work far more largely through combinations than where they live scattered and remote from one another. Many of us prefer the old conditions of life, under which the average man lived more to himself and by himself, where the average community was more self-dependent, and where even though the standard of comfort was lower on the average, yet there was less of the glaring inequality in worldly conditions which we now see about us in our great cities. It is not true that the poor have grown poorer; but some of the rich have grown so very much richer that, where multitudes of men are herded together in a limited space, the contrast strikes the onlooker as more violent than formerly. On the whole, our people earn more and live better than ever before, and the progress of which we are so proud could not have taken place had it not been for the upbuilding of industrial centres, such as this in which I am speaking.

But together with the good there has come a measure of evil. Life is not so simple as it was; and surely, both for the individual and the community, the simple life is normally the healthy life. There is not in the great cities the feeling of brotherhood which there is still in country localities; and the lines of social cleavage are far more deeply marked.

For some of the evils which have attended upon the good of the changed conditions we can at present see no complete remedy. For others the remedy must come by the action of men themselves in their private capacity, whether merely as individuals or by combination. For yet others some remedy can be found in legislative and executive action—national, State, or municipal. Much of the complaint against combinations is entirely unwarranted. Under present-day conditions it is as necessary to have corporations in the business world as it is to have organizations, unions, among wage-workers. We have a right to ask in each case only this: that good, and not harm, shall follow. Exactly as labor organizations, when managed intelligently and in a spirit of justice and fair play, are of very great service not only to the wage-workers, but to the whole community, as has been shown again and again in the history of many such organizations; so wealth, not merely individual, but corporate, when used aright is not merely beneficial to the community as a whole, but is absolutely essential to the up-building of such a series of communities as those whose citizens I am now addressing. This is so obvious that it ought to be too trite to mention, and yet it is necessary to mention it when we see some of the attacks made upon wealth, as such.

Of course a great fortune if used wrongly is a menace to the community. A man of great wealth who does not use that wealth decently is, in a peculiar sense, a menace to the community, and so is the man who does not use his intellect aright. Each talent—the talent for making money, the talent for showing intellect at the bar, or in any other way—if unaccompanied by character, makes the possessor a menace to the community. But such a fact no more warrants us in attacking wealth than it does in attacking intellect. Every man of power, by the very fact of that power, is capable of doing damage to his neighbors; but we cannot afford to discourage the development of such men merely because it is possible they may use their power for wrong ends. If we did so we should leave our history a blank, for we should have no great statesmen, soldiers, merchants, no great men of arts, of letters, of science. Doubtless on the average the most useful citizen to the community as a whole is the man to whom has been granted what the Psalmist asked for—neither poverty nor riches. But the great captain of industry, the man of wealth, who, alone or in combination with his fellows, drives through our great business enterprises, is a factor without whom the civilization that we see roundabout us here could not have been built up. Good, not harm, normally comes from the upbuilding of such wealth. Probably the greatest harm done by vast wealth is the harm that we of moderate means do ourselves when we let the vices of envy and hatred enter deep into our own natures.

But there is other harm; and it is evident that we should try to do away with that. The great corporations which we have grown to speak of rather loosely as trusts are the creatures of the State, and the State not only has the right to control them, but it is in duty bound to control them wherever the need of such control is shown. There is clearly need of supervision—need to possess the power of regulation of these great corporations through the representatives of the public—wherever, as in our own country at the present time, business corporations become so very powerful alike for beneficent work and for work that is not always beneficent. It is idle to say that there is no need for such supervision. There is, and a sufficient warrant for it is to be found in any one of the admitted evils appertaining to them.

We meet a peculiar difficulty under our system of government, because of the division of governmental power between the nation and the States. When the industrial conditions were simple, very little control was needed, and the difficulties of exercising such control under our Constitution were not evident. Now the conditions are complicated and we find it hard to frame national legislation which shall be adequate; while as a matter of practical experience it has been shown that the States either cannot or will not exercise a sufficient control to meet the needs of the case. Some of our States have excellent laws—laws which it would be well indeed to have enacted by the national legislature. But the wide-spread differences in these laws, even between ad-

jacent States, and the uncertainty of the power of enforcement, result practically in altogether insufficient control. I
believe that the nation must assume this power of control
by legislation; if necessary by constitutional amendment.
The immediate necessity in dealing with trusts is to place
them under the real, not the nominal, control of some sovereign to which, as its creatures, the trusts shall owe allegiance, and in whose courts the sovereign's orders may be
enforced.

This is not the case with the ordinary so-called "trust" to-
day; for the trust nowadays is a large State corporation,
which generally does business in other States, often with a
tendency toward monopoly. Such a trust is an artificial creature not wholly responsible to or controllable by any legislation, either by State or nation, and not subject to the
jurisdiction of any one court. Some governmental sovereign
must be given full power over these artificial, and very
powerful, corporate beings. In my judgment this sovereign
must be the National Government. When it has been given
full power, then this full power can be used to control any
evil influence, exactly as the government is now using the
power conferred upon it by the Sherman antitrust law.

Even when the power has been granted it would be most
unwise to exercise it too much, to begin by too stringent legislation. The mechanism of modern business is as delicate
and complicated as it is vast, and nothing would be more
productive of evil to all of us, and especially to those least
well off in this world's goods, than ignorant meddling with
this mechanism—above all, meddling in a spirit of class
legislation or hatred or rancor. It is eminently necessary that
the power should be had, but it is just as necessary that it
should be exercised with wisdom and self-restraint. The
first exercise of that power should be the securing of publicity among all great corporations doing an interstate business. The publicity, though non-inquisitorial, should be real

and thorough as to all important facts with which the public has concern. Daylight is a powerful discourager of evil.
Such publicity would by itself tend to cure the evils of
which there is just complaint; it would show us if evils existed, and where the evils are imaginary, and it would show
us what next ought to be done.

Above all, let us remember that our success in accomplishing anything depends very much upon our not trying
to accomplish everything. Distrust whoever pretends to
offer you a patent cure-all for every ill of the body politic,
just as you would a man who offers a medicine which
would cure every evil of your individual body. A medicine
that is recommended to cure both asthma and a broken leg
is not good for either. Mankind has moved slowly upward
through the ages, sometimes a little faster, sometimes a little slower, but rarely indeed by leaps and bounds. At times
a great crisis comes in which a great people, perchance led
by a great man, can at white heat strike some mighty blow
for the right—make a long stride in advance along the path
of justice and orderly liberty. But normally we must be content if each of us can do something—not all that we wish,
but something—for the advancement of those principles of
righteousness which underlie all real national greatness, all
true civilization and freedom. I see no promise of any immediate and complete solution of all the problems we
group together when we speak of the trust question. But we
can make a beginning in solving these problems, and a
good beginning, if only we approach the subject with a suf-
ficiency of resolution, of honesty, and of that hard common
sense which is one of the most valuable, and not always one
of the most common, assets in any nation's greatness. The
existing laws will be fully enforced as they stand on the
statute-books without regard to persons, and I think good
has already come from their enforcement. I think, furthermore, that additional legislation should be had and can be

had, which will enable us to accomplish much more along the same lines. No man can promise a perfect solution, at least in the immediate future. But something has already been done, and much more can be done if our people temperately and determinedly will that it shall be done.

In conclusion let me add one word. While we are not to be excused if we fail to do whatever is possible through the agency of government, we must keep ever in mind that no action of the government, no action by combination among ourselves, can take the place of the individual qualities to which in the long run every man must owe the success he can make of life. There never has been devised, and there never will be devised, any law which will enable a man to succeed save by the exercise of those qualities which have always been the prerequisites of success—the qualities of hard work, of keen intelligence, of unflinching will. Such action can supplement those qualities but it cannot take their place. No action by the State can do more than supplement the initiative of the individual; and ordinarily the action of the State can do no more than to secure to each individual the chance to show under as favorable conditions as possible the stuff that there is in him.

Liberty Under the Law

Ours is a government of liberty by, through, and under the law. No man is above it and no man is below it. The crime of cunning, the crime of greed, the crime of violence, are all equally crimes, and against them all alike the law must set its face. This is not and never shall be a government either of a plutocracy or of a mob. It is, it has been, and it will be, a government of the people including alike the people of

---

Speech at Spokane, Washington, May 26, 1903; in American Problems (Works, vol. 16)

great wealth and of moderate wealth, the people who employ others, the people who are employed; the wage-worker, the lawyer, the mechanic, the banker, the farmer; including them all, protecting each and every one if he acts decently and squarely, and discriminating against any one of them, no matter from what class he comes, if he does not act squarely and fairly, if he does not obey the law. While all people are foolish if they violate or rail against the law—wicked as well as foolish, but all foolish—yet the most foolish man in this Republic is the man of wealth who complains because the law is administered with impartial justice against or for him. His folly is greater than the folly of any other man who so complains; for he lives and moves and has his being because the law does in fact protect him and his property.

We have the right to ask every decent American citizen to rally to the support of the law if it is ever broken against the interest of the rich man; and we have the same right to ask that rich man cheerfully and gladly to acquiesce in the enforcement against his seeming interest of the law, if it is the law. Incidentally, whether he acquiesces or not, the law will be enforced, and this whoever he may be, great or small, and at whichever end of the social scale he may be.

I ask that we see to it in our country that the line of division in the deeper matters of our citizenship be drawn, never between section and section, never between creed and creed, never, thrice never, between class and class; but that the line be drawn on the line of conduct, cutting through sections, cutting through creeds, cutting through classes; the line that divides the honest from the dishonest, the line that divides good citizenship from bad citizenship, the line that declares a man a good citizen only if, and always if, he acts in accordance with the immutable law of righteousness, which has been the same from the beginning of history to the present moment, and which will be the same from now until the end of recorded time.

The Education of the Negro

To the white population as well as to the black, it is of the utmost importance that the negro be encouraged to make himself a citizen of the highest type of usefulness. It is to the interest of the white people that this policy be conscientiously pursued, and to the interest of the colored people that they clearly realize that they have opportunities for economic development here in the South not now offered elsewhere. Within the last twenty years the industrial operations of the South have increased so tremendously that there is a scarcity of labor almost everywhere; so that it is the part of wisdom for all who wish the prosperity of the South to help the negro to become in the highest degree useful to himself, and therefore to the community in which he lives. The South has always depended, and now depends, chiefly upon her native population for her work. Therefore in view of the scarcity not only of common labor, but of skilled labor, it becomes doubly important to train every available man to be of the utmost use, by developing his intelligence, his skill, and his capacity for conscientious effort. Hence the work of the Tuskegee Normal and Industrial Institute is a matter of the highest practical importance to both the white man and the black man, and well worth the support of both races alike in the South and in the North. Your fifteen hundred students are not only being educated in head and heart, but also trained to industrial efficiency, for from the beginning Tuskegee has placed especial emphasis upon the training of men and women in agriculture, mechanics, and household duties. Training in these three fundamental directions does not embrace all that the negro, or any other race, needs, but it does cover in a very

Address at Tuskegee Institute, Tuskegee, Alabama, October 24, 1905; in American Problems (Works, vol. 16)

large degree the field in which the negro can at present do most for himself and be most helpful to his white neighbors. Every black man who leaves this institute better able to do mechanical or industrial work adds by so much to the wealth of the whole community and benefits all people in the community. The professional and mercantile avenues to success are overcrowded; for the present the best chance of success awaits the intelligent worker at some mechanical trade or on a farm; for this man will almost certainly achieve industrial independence. I am pleased, but not in the least surprised, to learn that many among the men and women trained at Tuskegee find immediate employment as leaders and workers among their own people, and that their services are eagerly sought by white people for various kinds of industrial work, the demand being much greater than the supply. Viewed from any angle, ignorance is the costliest crop that can be raised in any part of this Union. Every dollar put into the education of either white man or black man, in head, in hand, and in heart, yields rich dividends to the entire community. Merely from the economic standpoint it is of the utmost consequence to all our citizens that institutions such as this at Tuskegee should be a success. But there are other and even higher reasons that entitle it to our support. In the interest of humanity, of justice, and of self-protection, every white man in America, no matter where he lives, should try to help the negro to help himself. It is in the interest and for the protection of the white man to see that the negro is educated. It is not only the duty of the white man, but it is to his interest, to see that the negro is protected in property, in life, and in all his legal rights. Every time a law is broken, every individual in the community has the moral tone of his life lowered. Lawlessness in the United States is not confined to any one section; lynching is not confined to any one section; and there is perhaps no body of American citizens who have deserved so well of the entire American people as the public men, the publicists, the clergymen, the countless thousands of high-minded private citizens, who have done such heroic work in the South in arousing public opinion against lawlessness in all its forms, and especially against lynching. I very earnestly hope that their example will count in the North as well as in the South, for there are just as great evils to be warred against in one region of our country as in another, though they are not in all places the same evils. And when any body of men in any community stands bravely for what is right, these men not merely serve a useful purpose in doing the particular task to which they set themselves, but give a lift to the cause of good citizenship throughout the Union. I heartily appreciate what you have done at Tuskegee; and I am sure you will not grudge my saying that it could not possibly have been done save for the loyal support you have received from the white people roundabout; for during the twenty-five years of effort to educate the black man here in the midst of a white community of intelligence and culture, there has never been an outbreak between the races, or any difficulty of any kind. All honor is due to the white men of Alabama, to the white men of Tuskegee, for what they have done. And right here let me say that if in any community a misunderstanding between the races arises, over any matter, infinitely the best way out is to have a prompt, frank, and full conference and consultation between representatives of the wise, decent, cool-headed men. Such a conference will always tend to bring about a better understanding, and will be a great help all round.

Hitherto I have spoken chiefly of the obligations existing on the part of the white man. Now remember on the other hand that no help can permanently avail you save as you yourselves develop capacity for self-help. You young colored men and women educated at Tuskegee must by precept and example lead your fellows toward sober, industrious, law-abiding lives. You are in honor bound to join hands in favor of law and order and to war against all crime, and especially against all crime by men of your own race; for the heaviest wrong done by the criminal is the wrong to his own race. You must teach the people of your race that they must scrupulously observe any contract into which they in good faith enter, no matter whether it is hard to keep or not. If you save money, secure homes, become taxpayers, and lead clean, decent, modest lives, you will win the respect of your neighbors of both races. Let each man strive to excel his fellows only by rendering substantial service to the community in which he lives. The colored people have many difficulties to pass through, but these difficulties will be surmounted if only the policy of reason and common sense is pursued. You have made real and great progress. According to the census the colored people of this country own and pay taxes upon something like three hundred million dollars' worth of property, and have blotted out over fifty per cent of their illiteracy. What you have done in the past is an indication of what you will be able to accomplish in the future under wise leadership. Moral and industrial education is what is most needed, in order that this progress may continue. The race cannot expect to get everything at once. It must learn to wait and bide its time; to prove itself worthy by showing its possession of perseverance, of thirst, of self-control. The destiny of the race is chiefly in its own hands, and must be worked out patiently and persistently along these lines. Remember also that the white man who can be of most use to the colored man is that colored man's neighbor. It is the Southern people themselves who must and can solve the difficulties that exist in the South; of course what help the people of the rest of the Union can give them must and will be gladly and cheerfully given. The hope of advancement for the colored man in the South lies in his steady, common-sense effort to improve his moral and material condition, and to work in harmony with the white man in upbuilding the Commonwealth. The future of the South now depends upon the people of both races living up to the spirit and letter of the laws of their several States and working out the destinies of both races, not as races, but as law-abiding American citizens.

The Nation and the States

I was very much pleased by your invitation to me to address you to-day. It is nearly twenty-nine years ago that I began my service in politics as a member of the Lower House of the New York State Legislature. I always felt that I graduated from Harvard, went into the New York Legislature, and began my education. I realize the great importance of the work of a state legislator, the difficulties under which he does that work, the temptations to which he is exposed; and I sympathize with the men who, having worked well, have the bitter knowledge that their good work has not been appreciated. If Colorado is at all like New York, there are occasional men who do not work well at all, and the extent of whose shortcomings should be practically appreciated more than it is. Since then, I have served in many different positions, including Governor and the position of Deputy Sheriff in the cow country under an employee of mine who was Sheriff; and, looking back, I can say with sincerity that I do not know any place where it is more necessary to have good work done, or where, together with bad work, there is more disinterested honest work done, than in the state legislatures of our country. Three or four gentlemen today have expressed the hope that I would speak to you about some of your own troubles. To relieve the obvi-

Speech before the Colorado Legislature, August 29, 1910; in The New Nationalism (Works, vol. 17) ous nervousness of the Assembly, I shall say that I am not going to do it, one reason being that, though each of those who addressed me felt very strongly that I should speak to you, each radically differed from all the others as to what I should say. There are troubles and failings connected with all legislative bodies about which I could speak; and of some of these I should speak to you now if I were not to make a speech this evening where I shall take them up at length.

I want now, as a man recently connected with the national government, to call attention to the great need that there shall be more coherent work in the future than in the past between the state and the national governments. The legislative and executive officers of our country, national and state, but, above all, the judicial officers, are to blame for the fact that there has grown up a neutral land—a borderland—in the spheres of action of the national and the state governments—a borderland over which each government tends to claim that it has the power, and as to which the action of the courts unfortunately has usually been such as to deny to both the power. Now, we have what I think is, on the whole, and with all its shortcomings and imperfections, the most satisfactory form of government that has yet been devised by men. I am accustomed to speak as a historian. There are plenty of defects in our system of government that I could point out; but, compared with the systems of government of other countries, good though some of them are, ours, I think, is the most satisfactory. One of the most valuable features is the largely realized effort to have the affairs that concern all of us throughout the land treated by the central or national legislature, while the affairs which concern us only in each of our several localities are treated by our state legislatures. That is the wisest possible method so long as no areas are left uncovered by them; so long as there are no spaces that are not filled in by government control.

Unfortunately, the course of governmental construction by the courts, as also the course of governmental action by legislator and executive, has not kept pace in this nation during the last forty years with the extraordinarily complex industrial development. We have changed from what was predominantly an agricultural people, where all were on planes of livelihood not far apart, and where business was simple, into a complex industrial community with a great development of corporations, and with conditions such that by steam and electricity the business of the nation has become completely nationalized. In consequence, the needs have wholly changed. There was no need, in the old days, of the law taking special care of the rights of the farm laborer; for he could take care of himself, and, if he was not treated right, he could move on and take up a farm himself. If he did not succeed on a farm, he could go to a city, or he could go West. But at present the relations of employer and employee are wholly different from what they were before. We now have to protect the employee to a degree unnecessary half a century ago. We now have to recognize the desirability of the right of collective bargaining on the part of the employees face to face with the great corporation, as was not necessary when the employer was one man or a partnership of two or three men employing half a dozen or half a score of men. So a hundred years ago, when the sailboat and the canal boat and the wagon and the pack train represented the only means of communication, the states could each take care of the business within the state. Now, as we have had to recognize in laws for the control of railroad business and of other interstate business, the national government is obliged to act.

It happens, probably inevitably, that the courts occupy a position of importance in our government such as they occupy in no other government, because, instead of dealing only with the rights of one man face to face with his fellow men, as is the case with other governments, they here pass upon the fundamental governmental rights of the whole people as exercised through their legislative and executive officers. Unfortunately, the courts, instead of leading in the recognition of the new conditions, have lagged behind; and, as each case has presented itself, have tended by a series of negative decisions to create a sphere in which neither nation nor state has effective control; and where the great business interests that can call to their aid the ability of the greatest corporation lawyers escape all control whatsoever. Let me illustrate what I mean by a reference to two concrete cases. Remember that I believe in state's rights wherever state's rights mean the people's rights. On the other hand, I believe in national rights wherever national rights mean the people's rights; and, above all, I believe that in every part of our complicated social fabric there must be either national or state control, and that it is ruinous to permit governmental action, and especially judicial action, which prevents the exercise of such control. I am for a fact, not a formula; I am for the rights of the people first and foremost, and for the "rights" of the nation or state, in any given series of cases, just in proportion as insistence upon them helps in securing popular rights.

The first case to which I shall refer is the Knight Sugar Trust case. In that case the Supreme Court of the United States handed down a decision which rendered it exceedingly difficult for the people to devise any method of controlling and regulating the business use of great capital in interstate commerce. It was a decision nominally against national rights, but really against popular rights—against the democratic principle of government by the people.

The second case is the so-called New York Bakeshop case. In New York City, as in most large cities, the baking business is likely to be carried on under unhygienic conditions—conditions which tell against the welfare of the general public. The New York Legislature passed, and the New York Governor signed, a bill remedying these unhealthy conditions. New York State was the only body which could deal with them; the nation had no power whatever in the matter. Acting on evidence which to them seemed ample and sufficient, acting in the interest of the public and in accordance with the demand of the public, the only governmental authority having affirmative power in the matter, the Governor, and the Legislature of the State of New York, took the action which they deemed necessary, after what inquiry and study was needed to satisfy them as to the conditions and as to the remedy. The Governor and the Legislature alone had the affirmative power to remedy the abuse. But the Supreme Court of the United States possessed— and, unfortunately, exercised—the negative power of not permitting the abuse to be remedied. By a five to four vote they declared the action of the State of New York unconstitutional, because, forsooth, men must not be deprived of their "liberty" to work under unhealthy conditions.

All who are acquainted with the effort to remedy industrial abuses know the type of mind (it may be perfectly honest but is absolutely fossilized) which declines to allow us to work for the betterment of conditions among the wage earners on the ground that we must not interfere with the "liberty" of a girl to work under conditions which jeopardize life and limb, or the "liberty" of a man to work under conditions which ruin his health after a limited number of years.

Such was the decision. The court was, of course, absolutely powerless to make the remotest attempt to provide a remedy for the wrong which undoubtedly existed, and its refusal to permit action by the state did not confer any power upon the nation to act. The decision was nominally against state's rights, really against popular rights.

Such decisions, arbitrarily and irresponsibly limiting the

power of the people, are of course fundamentally hostile to every species of real popular government. Representatives of the People of Colorado, here assembled in your legislative capacity, we as a nation should see to it that the people, through their several legislatures, national and state, have complete power of control in all matters that affect the public interest. There should be no means by which any man or set of men could escape the exercise of that control.

We should get the power; that is the first requisite. Now, then, the second is to see that the power be exercised with justice and moderation. The worst enemy of wise conservatism that I know is the type of conservative who tries to prevent wrongs from being remedied because the wrongs have existed for a long time; and, on the other hand, the worst enemy of true progress is the demagogue, or the visionary, who, in the name of progress, leads the people to make blunders such that in the resulting reaction they tend to distrust all progress. Distrust the demagogue and the mere visionary just as you distrust that hidebound conservative who too often, though an honest man himself, proves to be one of the most efficient friends of corruption. Remember that if you fall into the Scylla of demagogism, on the one hand, it will not help you that you have avoided the Charybdis of corruption and conservatism on the other. If you are in one gulf, it is perfectly true that you are not in the other. But you are in one.

Be progressive. A great democracy has got to be progressive, or it will soon cease to be either great or a democracy; but remember, no matter what your enthusiasm, that if you make rapid progress in the wrong direction you will merely have to undo it before you get to the right path again. As I have said before, each one of our localities has its own special problems to work out; and as to those special problems, an outsider is not competent to speak; but there are certain things to which all of us in every state should pay heed, we in New York and you in Colorado, the people of every state and the people of the national capital.

If I were asked to name the three influences which I thought were most dangerous to the perpetuity of American institutions, I should name corruption in business and politics alike, lawless violence, and mendacity, especially when used in connection with slander.

Corruption: You cannot afford to tolerate in your ranks the corrupt man, and the first duty of a constituency should be to see that its representative is not merely honest in the sense that he cannot be legally shown to be dishonest, but that he is a dead straight man whom no one can think of as crooked. I do not want it to be praise to a man that he is honest; I want it to be an impossible supposition for a representative to be thought of as anything else; but you cannot get that honesty unless you insist upon it among yourselves in your own relations of life. If you train up your children to hear a shady scoundrel spoken of with a certain half admiration as, "Well, he is smart"; if you let your children hear a man's crookedness excused on the ground that he is clever, that he is a cheat, but that he cheats mighty well, you have yourselves to blame if your legislatures betray you. More than that, distrust anything in the nature of class privilege; distrust the labor leader who will inveigh against corruption only when it is shown by the rich man; and distrust equally the rich man who will subscribe heavily to put down lawbreaking among small politicians, and who is shocked at corruption among labor leaders, but who leaves you instantly as soon as you try to bring the big corporation to book. If you elect a man because you think he will be honest towards your class,—capitalists, farmers, laborers,—and if you are indifferent as to whether he is honest towards other people, you can make up your minds absolutely that he will betray you if he gets the chance. You cannot afford not to have a man honest all the way through, because if he is not, you do not know quite where the breaking down will come.

Lawless violence: Here again remember that in time of mob violence all reform has to wait until order is restored. As a people it is gravely to our discredit that there should be so much unpunished murder, so many deeds of lawlessness and mob violence. Let the friend of the people who is severe upon the corruption of wealth make up his mind that he is a mighty poor public servant if he does not set his face against disorder when it takes the form of violence, just as much as against corruption. The man who can only see evil in the corruption of the rich, and the man who can only see evil in the lawless violence of the poor, stand on the same plane of bad citizenship. Keep order. War both against corruption and against lawless violence. That is what you and public officials need to keep in mind.

Now as to critics. I don't like the thief, but I like the liar just as little. The very fact that we need to have corruption in every phase unflinchingly exposed, the very fact that we need to have every man shown up who has acted improperly, because it is not merely a disgrace but a vital injury to us to permit corruption in public life or corruption in business life, that very fact emphasizes the wrong done by the man who without warrant accuses another of corruption. He has committed one of the cardinal sins against the body politic. It is not merely an injury to the man accused, it is an injury of the deepest type to the body politic, because after awhile, when accusations are continually and sweepingly made against all men, good and bad, the public as a whole grow to believe in each accusation a little and in no accusation entirely, so that they grow to believe that there is a little something bad about the decent man and that there is not much bad about the crook. No greater harm can be done to the body politic than by those men who, through reckless and indiscriminate accusation of good men and bad men, honest men and dishonest men alike, finally so hopelessly puzzle the public that they do not believe that any man in public life is entirely straight; while, on the other hand, they lose all indignation against the man who really is crooked. Greatly though I scorn and despise the corrupt public servant, greatly though I wish to see him punished with the utmost severity of the law, my scorn and contempt for him are no greater than for the man who by mendacity and through slander attacks the character of honest men just as he attacks the character of dishonest men, and thereby does his best, be that best great or small, to tear down the pillar of the temple and bury us all under the ruins. I speak of the man who writes in the daily press. (*Loud applause.*) I trust that it is not because this is a legislative assembly that you have applauded this more than what I said about public officials! Now, I will go with you to the last point in condemning the man who in the public press writes an untruth, if you will go with me to the last point in condemning equally actively the legislator who acts corruptly. Now, I will resume my sentence where I left off. I speak of the man who writes in the public press. I speak of the man who writes in the magazines. I speak of the politician on the stump. [*A pause—silence.*] Applaud! [*Loud applause.*] I knew I would get it when I pointed out the need of it! Judge men not by the class to which they belong, but by their conduct as individuals. The only man who I think is a little more useful than the wise and honest public official is the wise and honest man in the press, and the only man who I think is a little more noxious than the dishonest public official is the untruthful man in the public press. I will make myself perfectly clear. I ask you to stand by the official who is honest; I ask you to stand by the newspaper man and magazine writer who truthfully exposes corruption; and I ask you to stand against the official scoundrel who is dishonest and his equally base brother in the press who falsely accuses an honest man of dishonesty.

I thank you for the patience with which you have listened to me, and I am very glad I finally got all the applause I wanted at the points I wanted it.

The New Nationalism

We come here to-day to commemorate one of the epoch-making events of the long struggle for the rights of man—the long struggle for the uplift of humanity. Our country—this great republic—means nothing unless it means the triumph of a real democracy, the triumph of popular government, and, in the long run, of an economic system under which each man shall be guaranteed the opportunity to show the best that there is in him. That is why the history of America is now the central feature of the history of the world; for the world has set its face hopefully toward our democracy; and, O my fellow citizens, each one of you carries on your shoulders not only the burden of doing well for the sake of your own country, but the burden of doing well and of seeing that this nation does well for the sake of mankind.

There have been two great crises in our country's history: first, when it was formed, and then, again, when it was perpetuated; and, in the second of these great crises—in the time of stress and strain which culminated in the Civil War, on the outcome of which depended the justification of what had been done earlier, you men of the Grand Army, you men who fought through the Civil War, not only did you justify your generation, not only did you render life worth living for our generation, but you justified the wisdom of Washington and

Speech at Osawatomie, Kansas, August 31, 1910; in The New Nationalism (Works, vol. 17)

Washington's colleagues. If this republic had been founded by them only to be split asunder into fragments when the strain came, then the judgment of the world would have been that Washington's work was not worth doing. It was you who crowned Washington's work, as you carried to achievement the high purpose of Abraham Lincoln.

Now, with this second period of our history the name of John Brown will be forever associated; and Kansas was the theater upon which the first act of the second of our great national life dramas was played. It was the result of the struggle in Kansas which determined that our country should be in deed as well as in name devoted to both union and freedom; that the great experiment of democratic government on a national scale should succeed and not fail. In name we had the Declaration of Independence in 1776; but we gave the lie by our acts to the words of the Declaration of Independence until 1865; and words count for nothing except in so far as they represent acts. This is true everywhere; but, O my friends, it should be truest of all in political life. A broken promise is bad enough in private life. It is worse in the field of politics. No man is worth his salt in public life who makes on the stump a pledge which he does not keep after election; and, if he makes such a pledge and does not keep it, hunt him out of public life. I care for the great deeds of the past chiefly as spurs to drive us onward in the present. I speak of the men of the past partly that they may be honored by our praise of them, but more that they may serve as examples for the future.

It was a heroic struggle; and, as is inevitable with all such struggles, it had also a dark and terrible side. Very much was done of good, and much also of evil; and, as was inevitable in such a period of revolution, often the same man did both good and evil. For our great good fortune as a nation, we, the people of the United States as a whole, can now afford to forget the evil, or, at least, to remember it without bitterness, and to fix our eyes with pride only on the good that was accomplished. Even in ordinary times there are very few of us who do not see the problems of life as through a glass, darkly; and when the glass is clouded by the murk of furious popular passion, the vision of the best and the bravest is dimmed. Looking back, we are all of us now able to do justice to the valor and the disinterestedness and the love of the right, as to each it was given to see the right, shown both by the men of the North and the men of the South in that contest which was finally decided by the attitude of the West. We can admire the heroic valor, the sincerity, the self-devotion shown alike by the men who wore the blue and the men who wore the gray; and our sadness that such men should have had to fight one another is tempered by the glad knowledge that ever hereafter their descendants shall be found fighting side by side, struggling in peace as well as in war for the uplift of their common country, all alike resolute to raise to the highest pitch of honor and usefulness the nation to which they all belong. As for the veterans of the Grand Army of the Republic, they deserve honor and recognition such as is paid to no other citizens of the republic; for to them the republic owes its all; for to them it owes its very existence. It is because of what you and your comrades did in the dark years that we of to-day walk, each of us, head erect, and proud that we belong, not to one of a dozen little squabbling contemptible commonwealths, but to the mightiest nation upon which the sun shines.

I do not speak of this struggle of the past merely from the historic standpoint. Our interest is primarily in the application to-day of the lessons taught by the contest of half a century ago. It is of little use for us to pay lip loyalty to the mighty men of the past unless we sincerely endeavor to apply to the problems of the present precisely the qualities which in other crises enabled the men of that day to meet those crises. It is half melancholy and half amusing to see the way in which well-meaning people gather to do honor to the men who, in company with John Brown, and under the lead of Abraham Lincoln, faced and solved the great problems of the nineteenth century, while, at the same time, these same good people nervously shrink from, or frantically denounce, those who are trying to meet the problems of the twentieth century in the spirit which was accountable for the successful solution of the problems of Lincoln's time.

Of that generation of men to whom we owe so much, the man to whom we owe most is, of course, Lincoln. Part of our debt to him is because he forecast our present struggle and saw the way out. He said:—

> I hold that while man exists it is his duty to improve not only his own condition, but to assist in ameliorating mankind.

And again:—

> Labor is prior to, and independent of, capital. Capital is only the fruit of labor, and could never have existed if labor had not first existed. Labor is the superior of capital, and deserves much the higher consideration.

If that remark was original with me, I should be even more strongly denounced as a communist agitator than I shall be anyhow. It is Lincoln's. I am only quoting it; and that is one side; that is the side the capitalist should hear. Now, let the workingman hear his side.

> Capital has its rights, which are as worthy of protection as any other rights. . . . Not should this lead to a war upon the owners of property. Property is the fruit of labor; . . . property is desirable; is a positive good in the world.

And then comes a thoroughly Lincolnlike sentence:—

Let not him who is houseless pull down the house of another, but let him work diligently and build one for himself, thus by example assuring that his own shall be safe from violence when built.

It seems to me that, in these words, Lincoln took substantially the attitude that we ought to take; he showed the proper sense of proportion in his relative estimates of capital and labor, of human rights and property rights. Above all, in this speech, as in many others, he taught a lesson in wise kindliness and charity; an indispensable lesson to us of to-day. But this wise kindliness and charity never weakened his arm or numbed his heart. We cannot afford weakly to blind ourselves to the actual conflict which faces us to-day. The issue is joined, and we must fight or fail.

In every wise struggle for human betterment one of the main objects, and often the only object, has been to achieve in large measure equality of opportunity. In the struggle for this great end, nations rise from barbarism to civilization, and through it people press forward from one stage of enlightenment to the next. One of the chief factors in progress is the destruction of special privilege. The essence of any struggle for healthy liberty has always been, and must always be, to take from some one man or class of men the right to enjoy power, or wealth, or position, or immunity, which has not been earned by service to his or their fellows. That is what you fought for in the Civil War, and that is what we strive for now.

At many stages in the advance of humanity, this conflict between the men who possess more than they have earned and the men who have earned more than they possess is the central condition of progress. In our day it appears as the struggle of free men to gain and hold the right of self-government as against the special interests, who twist the methods of free government into machinery for defeating

the popular will. At every stage, and under all circumstances, the essence of the struggle is to equalize opportunity, destroy privilege, and give to the life and citizenship of
every individual the highest possible value both to himself
and to the commonwealth. That is nothing new. All I ask in
civil life is what you fought for in the Civil War. I ask that
civil life be carried on according to the spirit in which the
army was carried on. You never get perfect justice, but
the effort in handling the army was to bring to the front the
men who could do the job. Nobody grudged promotion to
Grant, or Sherman, or Thomas, or Sheridan, because they
earned it. The only complaint was when a man got promotion, which he did not earn.

Practical equality of opportunity for all citizens, when we
achieve it, will have two great results. First, every man will
have a fair chance to make of himself all that in him lies; to
reach the highest point to which his capacities, unassisted
by special privilege of his own and unhampered by the special privilege of others, can carry him, and to get for himself
and his family substantially what he has earned. Second,
equality of opportunity means that the commonwealth will
get from every citizen the highest service of which he is capable. No man who carries the burden of the special privileges of another can give to the commonwealth that service
to which it is fairly entitled.

I stand for the square deal. But when I say that I am for
the square deal, I mean not merely that I stand for fair play
under the present rules of the game, but that I stand for
having those rules changed so as to work for a more substantial equality of opportunity and of reward for equally
good service. One word of warning, which, I think, is
hardly necessary in Kansas. When I say I want a square deal
for the poor man, I do not mean that I want a square deal
for the man who remains poor because he has not got the
energy to work for himself. If a man who has had a chance

will not make good, then he has got to quit. And you men of the Grand Army, you want justice for the brave man who fought, and punishment for the coward who shirked his work. Is not that so?

Now, this means that our government, national and state, must be freed from the sinister influence or control of special interests. Exactly as the special interests of cotton and slavery threatened our political integrity before the Civil War, so now the great special business interests too often control and corrupt the men and methods of government for their own profit. We must drive the special interests out of politics. That is one of our tasks to-day. Every special interest is entitled to justice—full, fair, and complete,—and, now, mind you, if there were any attempt by mob violence to plunder and work harm to the special interest, whatever it may be, that I most dislike, and the wealthy man, whomsoever he may be, for whom I have the greatest contempt, I would fight for him, and you would if you were worth your salt. He should have justice. For every special interest is entitled to justice, but not one is entitled to a vote in Congress, to a voice on the bench, or to representation in any public office. The Constitution guarantees protection to property, and we must make that promise good. But it does give the right of suffrage to any corporation.

The true friend of property, the true conservative, is he who insists that property shall be the servant and not the master of the commonwealth; who insists that the creature of man's making shall be the servant and not the master of the man who made it. The citizens of the United States must effectively control the mighty commercial forces which they have themselves called into being.

There can be no effective control of corporations while their political activity remains. To put an end to it will be neither a short nor an easy task, but it can be done.

We must have complete and effective publicity of corporate affairs, so that the people may know beyond peradventure whether the corporations obey the law and whether their management entitles them to the confidence of the public. It is necessary that laws should be passed to prohibit the use of corporate funds directly or indirectly for political purposes; it is still more necessary that such laws should be thoroughly enforced. Corporate expenditures for political purposes, and especially such expenditures by public service corporations, have supplied one of the principal sources of corruption in our political affairs.

It has become entirely clear that we must have government supervision of the capitalization, not only of public service corporations, including, particularly, railways, but of all corporations doing an interstate business. I do not wish to see the nation forced into the ownership of the railways if it can possibly be avoided, and the only alternative is thoroughgoing and effective regulation, which shall be based on a full knowledge of all the facts, including a physical valuation of property. This physical valuation is not needed, or, at least, is very rarely needed, for fixing rates; but it is needed as the basis of honest capitalization.

We have come to recognize that franchises should never be granted except for a limited time, and never without proper provision for compensation to the public. It is my personal belief that the same kind and degree of control and supervision which should be exercised over public service corporations should be extended also to combinations which control necessaries of life, such as meat, oil, and coal, or which deal in them on an important scale. I have no doubt that the ordinary man who has control of them is much like ourselves. I have no doubt he would like to do well, but I want to have enough supervision to help him realize that desire to do well.

I believe that the officers, and, especially, the directors, of corporations should be held personally responsible when any corporation breaks the law.

Combinations in industry are the result of an imperative economic law which cannot be repealed by political legislation. The effort at prohibiting all combination has substantially failed. The way out lies, not in attempting to prevent such combinations, but in completely controlling them in the interest of the public welfare. For that purpose the Federal Bureau of Corporations is an agency of first importance. Its powers, and, therefore, its efficiency, as well as that of the Interstate Commerce Commission, should be largely increased. We have a right to expect from the Bureau of Corporations and from the Interstate Commerce Commission a very high grade of public service. We should be as sure of the proper conduct of the interstate railways and the proper management of interstate business as we are now sure of the conduct and management of the national banks, and we should have as effective supervision in one case as in the other. The Hepburn Act, and the amendment to the Act in the shape in which it finally passed Congress at the last session, represent a long step in advance, and we must go yet further.

There is a widespread belief among our people that, under the methods of making tariffs which have hitherto obtained, the special interests are too influential. Probably this is true of both the big special interests and the little special interests. These methods have put a premium on selfishness, and, naturally, the selfish big interests have gotten more than their smaller, though equally selfish, brothers. The duty of Congress is to provide a method by which the interest of the whole people shall be all that receives consideration. To this end there must be an expert tariff commission, wholly removed from the possibility of political pressure or of improper business influence. Such a commission can find the real difference between cost of production, which is mainly the difference of labor cost here and abroad. As fast as its recommendations are made, I believe in revising one schedule at a time. A general revision of the tariff almost inevitably leads to log-rolling and the subordination of the general public interest to local and special interests.

The absence of effective state, and, especially, national, restraint upon unfair money getting has tended to create a small class of enormously wealthy and economically powerful men, whose chief object is to hold and increase their power. The prime need is to change the conditions which enable these men to accumulate power which it is not for the general welfare that they should hold or exercise. We grudge no man a fortune which represents his own power and sagacity, when exercised with entire regard to the welfare of his fellows. Again, comrades over there, take the lesson from your own experience. Not only did you not grudge, but you gloried in the promotion of the great generals who gained their promotion by leading the army to victory. So it is with us. We grudge no man a fortune in civil life if it is honorably obtained and well used. It is not even enough that it should have been gained without doing damage to the community. We should permit it to be gained only so long as the gaining represents benefit to the community. This, I know, implies a policy of a far more active governmental interference with social and economic conditions in this country than we have yet had, but I think we have got to face the fact that such an increase in governmental control is now necessary.

No man should receive a dollar unless that dollar has been fairly earned. Every dollar received should represent a dollar's worth of service rendered—not gambling in stocks, but service rendered. The really big fortune, the swollen fortune, by the mere fact of its size acquires qualities which differentiate it in kind as well as in degree from what is possessed by men of relatively small means. Therefore, I believe in a graduated income tax on big fortunes, and in another tax which is far more easily collected and far more effective—a graduated inheritance tax on big fortunes, properly safeguarded against evasion and increasing rapidly in amount with the size of the estate.

The people of the United States suffer from periodical financial panics to a degree substantially unknown among the other nations which approach us in financial strength. There is no reason why we should suffer what they escape. It is of profound importance that our financial system should be promptly investigated, and so thoroughly and effectively revised as to make it certain that hereafter our currency will no longer fail at critical times to meet our needs.

It is hardly necessary for me to repeat that I believe in an efficient army and a navy large enough to secure for us abroad that respect which is the surest guarantee of peace. A word of special warning to my fellow citizens who are as progressive as I hope I am. I want them to keep up their interest in our internal affairs; and I want them also continually to remember Uncle Sam's interests abroad. Justice and fair dealing among nations rest upon principles identical with those which control justice and fair dealing among the individuals of which nations are composed, with the vital exception that each nation must do its own part in international police work. If you get into trouble here, you can call for the police; but if Uncle Sam gets into trouble, he has got to be his own policeman, and I want to see him strong enough to encourage the peaceful aspirations of other peoples in connection with us. I believe in national friendships and heartiest good will to all nations; but national friendships, like those between men, must be founded on respect as well as on liking, on forbearance as well as upon trust. I should be heartily ashamed of any American who did not try to make the American government act as justly toward the other nations in international relations as he himself would act toward any individual in private relations. I should be heartily ashamed to see us wrong a weaker power, and I should hang my head forever if we tamely suffered wrong from a stronger power.

Of conservation I shall speak more at length elsewhere. Conservation means development as much as it does protection. I recognize the right and duty of this generation to develop and use the natural resources of our land; but I do not recognize the right to waste them, or to rob, by wasteful use, the generations that come after us. I ask nothing of the nation except that it so behave as each farmer here behaves with reference to his own children. That farmer is a poor creature who skins the land and leaves it worthless to his children. The farmer is a good farmer who, having enabled the land to support himself and to provide for the education of his children, leaves it to them a little better than he found it himself. I believe the same thing of a nation.

Moreover, I believe that the natural resources must be used for the benefit of all our people, and not monopolized for the benefit of the few, and here again is another case in which I am accused of taking a revolutionary attitude. People forget now that one hundred years ago there were public men of good character who advocated the nation selling its public lands in great quantities, so that the nation could get the most money out of it, and giving it to the men who could cultivate it for their own uses. We took the proper democratic ground that the land should be granted in small sections to the men who were actually to till it and live on it. Now, with the water power, with the forests, with the mines, we are brought face to face with the fact that there are many people who will go with us in conserving the resources only if they are to be allowed to exploit them for their benefit. That is one of the fundamental reasons why the special interests should be driven out of politics. Of all the questions which can come before this nation, short of the actual preservation of its existence in a great war, there is none which compares in importance with the great central task of leaving this land even a better land for our descendants than it is for us, and training them into a better race to inhibit the land and pass it on. Conservation is a great moral issue, for it involves the patriotic duty of insuring the safety and continuance of the nation. Let me add that the health and vitality of our people are at least as well worth conserving as their forests, waters, lands, and minerals, and in this great work the national government must bear a most important part.

I have spoken elsewhere also of the great task which lies before the farmers of the country to get for themselves and their wives and children not only the benefits of better farming, but also those of better business methods and better conditions of life on the farm. The burden of this great task will fall, as it should, mainly upon the great organizations of the farmers themselves. I am glad it will, for I believe they are all well able to handle it. In particular, there are strong reasons why the Departments of Agriculture of the various states, the United States Department of Agriculture, and the agricultural colleges and experiment stations should extend their work to cover all phrases of farm life, instead of limiting themselves, as they have far too often limited themselves in the past, solely to the question of the production of crops. And now a special word to the farmer. I want to see him make the farm as fine a farm as it can be made; and let him remember to see that the improvement goes on indoors as well as out; let him remember that the farmer's wife should have her share of thought and attention just as much as the farmer himself.

Nothing is more true than that excess of every kind is followed by reaction; a fact which should be pondered by reformer and reactionary alike. We are face to face with conceptions of the relations of property to human welfare, chiefly because certain advocates of the rights of property as against the rights of men have been pushing their claims too far. The man who wrongly holds that every human right is secondary to his profit must now give way to the advocate of human welfare, who rightly maintains that every man holds his property subject to the general right of the community to regulate its use to whatever degree the public welfare may require it.

But I think we may go still further. The right to regulate the use of wealth in the public interest is universally admitted. Let us admit also the right to regulate the terms and conditions of labor, which is the chief element of wealth, directly in the interest of the common good. The fundamental thing to do for every man is to give him a chance to reach a place in which he will make the greatest possible contribution to the public welfare. Understand what I say there. Give him a chance, not push him up if he will not be pushed. Help any man who stumbles; if he lies down, it is a poor job to try to carry him; but if he is a worthy man, try your best to see that he gets a chance to show the worth that is in him. No man can be a good citizen unless he has a wage more than sufficient to cover the bare cost of living, and hours of labor short enough so that after his day's work is done he will have time and energy to bear his share in the management of the community, to help in carrying the general load. We keep countless men from being good citizens by the conditions of life with which we surround them. We need comprehensive workmen's compensation acts, both state and national laws to regulate child labor and work for women, and, especially, we need in our common schools not merely education in book learning, but also practical training for daily life and work. We need to enforce better sanitary conditions for our workers and to extend the use of safety appliances for our workers in industry and commerce, both within and between the states. Also, friends, in the interest of the workingman himself we need to set our faces like flint against mob violence just as against corporate greed; against violence and injustice and lawlessness by wage workers just as much as against lawless cunning and greed and selfish arrogance of employers. If I could ask but one thing of my fellow countrymen, my request would be that, whenever they go in for reform, they remember the two sides, and that they always exact justice from one side as much as from the other. I have small use for the public servant who can always see and denounce the corruption of the capitalist, but who cannot persuade himself, especially before election, to say a word about lawless mob violence. And I have equally small use for the man, be he a judge on the bench, or editor of a great paper, or wealthy and influential private citizen, who can see clearly enough and denounce the lawlessness of mob violence, but whose eyes are closed so that he is blind when the question is one of corruption in business on a gigantic scale. Also remember what I said about excess in reformer and reactionary alike. If the reactionary man, who thinks of nothing but the rights of property, could have his way, he would bring about a revolution; and one of my chief fears in connection with progress comes because I do not want to see our people, for lack of proper leadership, compelled to follow men whose intentions are excellent, but whose eyes are a little too wild to make it really safe to trust them. Here in Kansas there is one paper which habitually denounces me as the tool of Wall Street, and at the same time frantically repudiates the statement that I am a Socialist on the ground that that is an unwarranted slander of the Socialists.

National efficiency has many factors. It is a necessary result of the principle of conservation widely applied. In the end it will determine our failure or success as a nation.

National efficiency has to do, not only with natural resources and with men, but it is equally concerned with institutions. The state must be made efficient for the work
which concerns only the people of the state; and the nation
for that which concerns all the people. There must remain
no neutral ground to serve as a refuge for lawbreakers, and
especially for lawbreakers of great wealth, who can hire the
vulpine legal cunning which will teach them how to avoid
both jurisdictions. It is a misfortune when the national legislature fails to do its duty in providing a national remedy,
so that the only national activity is the purely negative activity of the judiciary in forbidding the state to exercise
power in the premises.

I do not ask for overcentralization; but I do ask that we
work in a spirit of broad and far-reaching nationalism when
we work for what concerns our people as a whole. We are
all Americans. Our common interests are as broad as the
continent. I speak to you here in Kansas exactly as I would
speak in New York or Georgia, for the most vital problems
are those which affect us all alike. The national government
belongs to the whole American people, and where the
whole American people are interested, that interest can be
guarded effectively only by the national government. The
betterment which we seek must be accomplished, I believe,
mainly through the national government.

The American people are right in demanding that New
Nationalism, without which we cannot hope to deal with
new problems. The New Nationalism puts the national
need before sectional or personal advantage. It is impatient
of the utter confusion that results from local legislatures attempting to treat national issues as local issues. It is still
more impatient of the impotence which springs from over-
division of governmental powers, the impotence which
makes it possible for local selfishness or for legal cunning,
hired by wealthy special interests, to bring national activi-

ties to a deadlock. This New Nationalism regards the executive power as the steward of the public welfare. It demands of the judiciary that it shall be interested primarily in human welfare rather than in property, just as it demands that the representative body shall represent all the people rather than any one class or section of the people.

I believe in shaping the ends of government to protect property as well as human welfare. Normally, and in the long run, the ends are the same; but whenever the alternative must be faced, I am for men and not for property, as you were in the Civil War. I am far from underestimating the importance of dividends; but I rank dividends below human character. Again, I do not have any sympathy with the reformer who says he does not care for dividends. Of course, economic welfare is necessary, for a man must pull his own weight and be able to support his family. I know well that the reformers must not bring upon the people economic ruin, or the reforms themselves will go down in the ruin. But we must be ready to face temporary disaster, whether or not brought on by those who will war against us to the knife. Those who oppose all reform will do well to remember that ruin in its worst form is inevitable if our national life brings us nothing better than swollen fortunes for the few and the triumph in both politics and business of a sordid and selfish materialism.

If our political institutions were perfect, they would absolutely prevent the political domination of money in any part of our affairs. We need to make our political representatives more quickly and sensitively responsive to the people whose servants they are. More direct action by the people in their own affairs under proper safeguards is vitally necessary. The direct primary is a step in this direction, if it is associated with a corrupt practices act effective to prevent the advantage of the man willing recklessly and unscrupulously to spend money over his more honest competitor. It is particularly important that all moneys received or expended for campaign purposes should be publicly accounted for, not only after election, but before election as well. Political action must be made simpler, easier, and freer from confusion for every citizen. I believe that the prompt removal of unfaithful or incompetent public servants should be made easy and sure in whatever way experience shall show to be most expedient in any given class of cases.

One of the fundamental necessities in a representative government such as ours is to make certain that the men to whom the people delegate their power shall serve the people by whom they are elected, and not the special interests. I believe that every national officer, elected or appointed, should be forbidden to perform any service or receive any compensation, directly or indirectly, from interstate corporations; and a similar provision could not fail to be useful within the states.

The object of government is the welfare of the people. The material progress and prosperity of a nation are desirable chiefly so far as they lead to the moral and material welfare of all good citizens. Just in proportion as the average man and woman are honest, capable of sound judgment and high ideals, active in public affairs,—but, first of all, sound in their home life, and the father and mother of healthy children whom they bring up well,—just so far, and no farther, we may count our civilization a success. We must have—I believe we have already—a genuine and permanent moral awakening, without which no wisdom of legislation or administration really means anything; and, on the other hand, we must try to secure the social and economic legislation without which any improvement due to purely moral agitation is necessarily evanescent. Let me again illustrate by a reference to the Grand Army. You could not have won simply as a disorderly and disorganized mob. You needed generals; you needed careful administration of the most advanced type; and a good commissary—the cracker line. You well remember that success was necessary in many different lines in order to bring about general success. You had to have the administration at Washington good, just as you had to have the administration in the field; and you had to have the work of the generals good. You could not have triumphed without that administration and leadership; but it would all have been worthless if the average soldier had not had the right stuff in him. He had to have the right stuff in him, or you could not get it out of him. In the last analysis, therefore, vitally necessary though it was to have the right kind of organization and the right kind of generalship, it was even more vitally necessary that the average soldier should have the fighting edge, the right character. So it is in our civil life. No matter how honest and decent we are in our private lives, if we do not have the right kind of law and the right kind of administration of the law, we cannot go forward as a nation. That is imperative; but it must be an addition to, and not a substitution for, the qualities that make us good citizens. In the last analysis, the most important elements in any man's career must be the sum of those qualities which, in the aggregate, we speak of as character. If he has not got it, then no law that the wit of man can devise, no administration of the law by the boldest and strongest executive, will avail to help him. We must have the right kind of character—character that makes a man, first of all, a good man in the home, a good father, a good husband—that makes a man a good neighbor. You must have that, and, then, in addition, you must have the kind of law and the kind of administration of the law which will give to those qualities in the private citizen the best possible chance for development. The prime problem of our nation is to get the right type of good citizenship, and, to get it, we must have progress, and our public men must be genuinely progressive.

The Right of the People to Rule

The great fundamental issue now before the Republican party and before our people can be stated briefly. It is, Are the American people fit to govern themselves, to rule themselves, to control themselves? I believe they are. My opponents do not. I believe in the right of the people to rule. I believe the majority of the plain people of the United States will, day in and day out, make fewer mistakes in governing themselves than any smaller class or body of men, no matter what their training, will make in trying to govern them. I believe, again, that the American people are, as a whole, capable of self-control and of learning by their mistakes. Our opponents pay lip-loyalty to this doctrine; but they show their real beliefs by the way in which they champion every device to make the nominal rule of the people a sham.

I have scant patience with this talk of the tyranny of the majority. Wherever there is tyranny of the majority, I shall protest against it with all my heart and soul. But we are today suffering from the tyranny of minorities. It is a small minority that is grabbing our coal-deposits, our water-powers, and our harbor fronts. A small minority is battening on the sale of adulterated foods and drugs. It is a small minority that lies behind monopolies and trusts. It is a small minority that stands behind the present law of master and servant, the sweat shops, and the whole calendar of social and industrial injustice. It is a small minority that is to-day using our convention system to defeat the will of a majority of the people in the choice of delegates to the Chicago Convention.

The only tyrannies from which men, women, and children are suffering in real life are the tyrannies of minorities.

Address at Carnegie Hall, New York City, March 20, 1912; in Progressive Principles (Works, vol. 17)

If the majority of the American people were in fact tyrannous over the minority, if democracy had no greater self-control than empire, then indeed no written words which our forefathers put into the Constitution could stay that tyranny.

No sane man who has been familiar with the government of this country for the last twenty years will complain that we have had too much of the rule of the majority. The trouble has been a far different one—that, at many times and in many localities, there have held public office in the States and in the nation men who have, in fact, served not the whole people, but some special class or special interest. I am not thinking only of those special interests which by grosser methods, by bribery and crime, have stolen from the people. I am thinking as much of their respectable allies and figureheads, who have ruled and legislated and decided as if in some way the vested rights of privilege had a first mortgage on the whole United States, while the rights of all the people were merely an unsecured debt.

Am I overstating the case? Have our political leaders always, or generally, recognized their duty to the people as anything more than a duty to disperse the mob, see that the ashes are taken away, and distribute patronage? Have our leaders always, or generally, worked for the benefit of human beings, to increase the prosperity of all the people, to give to each some opportunity of living decently and bringing up his children well? The questions need no answer.

Now there has sprung up a feeling deep in the hearts of the people—not of the bosses and professional politicians, not of the beneficiaries of special privilege—a pervading belief of thinking men that when the majority of the people do in fact, as well as theory, rule, then the servants of the people will come more quickly to answer and obey, not the commands of the special interests, but those of the whole people. To reach toward that end the Progressives of the Republican party in certain States have formulated certain proposals for change in the form of the State government—certain new "checks and balances" which may check and balance the special interests and their allies. That is their purpose. Now turn for a moment to their proposed methods.

First, there are the "initiative and referendum," which are so framed that if the legislatures obey the command of some special interest, and obstinately refuse the will of the majority, the majority may step in and legislate directly. No man would say that it was best to conduct all legislation by direct vote of the people—it would mean the loss of deliberation, of patient consideration—but, on the other hand, no one whose mental arteries have not long since hardened can doubt that the proposed changes are needed when the legislatures refuse to carry out the will of the people. The proposal is a method to reach an undeniable evil. Then there is the recall of public officers—the principle that an officer chosen by the people who is unfaithful may be recalled by vote of the majority before he finishes his term. I will speak of the recall of judges in a moment—leave that aside—but as to the other officers, I have heard no argument advanced against the proposition, save that it will make the public officer timid and always currying favor with the mob. That argument means that you can fool all the people all the time, and is an avowal of disbelief in democracy. If it be true—and I believe it is not—it is less important than to stop those public officers from currying favor with the interests. Certain States may need the recall, others may not; where the term of elective office is short it may be quite needless; but there are occasions when it meets a real evil, and provides a needed check and balance against the special interests.

Then there is the direct primary—the real one, not the

New York one—and that, too, the Progressives offer as a check on the special interests. Most clearly of all does it seem to me that this change is wholly good—for every State. The system of party government is not written in our constitutions, but it is none the less a vital and essential part of our form of government. In that system the party leaders should serve and carry out the will of their own party. There is no need to show how far that theory is from the facts, or to rehearse the vulgar thieving partnerships of the corporations and the bosses, or to show how many times the real government lies in the hands of the boss, protected from the commands and the revenge of the voters by his puppets in office and the power of patronage. We need not be told how he is thus intrenched nor how hard he is to overthrow. The facts stand out in the history of nearly every State in the Union. They are blots on our political system. The direct primary will give the voters a method ever ready to use, by which the party leader shall be made to obey their command. The direct primary, if accompanied by a stringent corrupt-practices act, will help break up the corrupt partnership of corporations and politicians.

My opponents charge that two things in my programme are wrong because they intrude into the sanctuary of the judiciary. The first is the recall of judges; and the second, the review by the people of judicial decisions on certain constitutional questions.

I have said again and again that I do not advocate the recall of judges in all States and in all communities. In my own State I do not advocate it or believe it to be needed, for in this State our trouble lies not with corruption on the bench, but with the effort by the honest but wrong-headed judges to thwart the people in their struggle for social justice and fair dealing. The integrity of our judges from Marshall to White and Holmes—and to Cullen and many others in our own State—is a fine page of American history.

But—I say it soberly—democracy has a right to approach the sanctuary of the courts when a special interest has corruptly found sanctuary there; and this is exactly what has happened in some of the States where the recall of the judges is a living issue. I would far more willingly trust the whole people to judge such a case than some special tribunal—perhaps appointed by the same power that chose the judge—if that tribunal is not itself really responsible to the people and is hampered and clogged by the technicalities of impeachment proceedings.

I have stated that the courts of the several States—not always but often—have construed the "due process" clause of the State constitutions as if it prohibited the whole people of the State from adopting methods of regulating the use of property so that human life, particularly the lives of the working men, shall be safer, freer, and happier. No one can successfully impeach this statement. I have insisted that the true construction of "due process" is that pronounced by Justice Holmes in delivering the unanimous opinion of the Supreme Court of the United States, when he said:

"The police power extends to all the great public need. It may be put forth in aid of what is sanctioned by usage, or held by the prevailing morality or strong and preponderant opinion to be greatly and immediately necessary to the public welfare."

I insist that the decision of the New York court of appeals in the Ives case, which set aside the will of the majority of the people as to the compensation of injured workmen in dangerous trades, was intolerable and based on a wrong political philosophy. I urge that in such cases where the courts construe the due process clause as if property rights, to the exclusion of human rights, had a first mortgage on the Constitution, the people may, after sober deliberation, vote, and finally determine whether the law which the court set aside shall be valid or not. By this method can be clearly and finally ascertained the preponderant opinion of the people which Justice Holmes makes the test of due process in the case of laws enacted in the exercise of the police power. The ordinary methods now in vogue of amending the Constitution have in actual practice proved wholly inadequate to secure justice in such cases with reasonable speed, and cause intolerable delay and injustice, and those who stand against the changes I propose are champions of wrong and injustice, and of tyranny by the wealthy and the strong over the weak and the helpless.

So that no man may misunderstand me, let me recapitulate:

(1) I am not proposing anything in connection with the Supreme Court of the United States, or with the Federal Constitution.

(2) I am not proposing anything having any connection with ordinary suits, civil or criminal, as between individuals.

(3) I am not speaking of the recall of judges.

(4) I am proposing merely that in a certain class of cases involving police power, when a State court has set aside as unconstitutional a law passed by the legislature for the general welfare, the question of the validity of the law—which should depend, as Justice Holmes so well phrases it, upon the prevailing morality or preponderant opinion—be submitted for final determination to a vote of the people, taken after due time for consideration.

And I contend that the people, in the nature of things, must be better judges of what is the preponderant opinion than the courts, and that the courts should not be allowed to reverse the political philosophy of the people. My point is well illustrated by a recent decision of the Supreme Court, holding that the court would not take jurisdiction of a case involving the constitutionality of the initiative and referendum laws of Oregon. The ground of the decision was that such a question was not judicial in its nature, but should be left for determination to the other co-ordinate departments of the government. Is it not equally plain that the question whether a given social policy is for the public good is not of a judicial nature, but should be settled by the legislature, or in the final instance by the people themselves?

The President of the United States, Mr. Taft, devoted most of a recent speech to criticism of this proposition. He says that it "is utterly without merit or utility, and, instead of being . . . in the interest of all the people, and of the stability of popular government, is sowing the seeds of confusion and tyranny." (By this he, of course, means the tyranny of the majority, that is, the tyranny of the American people as a whole.) He also says that my proposal (which, as he rightly sees, is merely a proposal to give the people a real, instead of only a nominal, chance to construe and amend a State constitution with reasonable rapidity) would make such amendment and interpretation "depend on the feverish, uncertain, and unstable determination of successive votes on different laws by temporary and changing majorities"; and that "it lays the axe at the root of the tree of well-ordered freedom, and subjects the guaranties of life, liberty, and property without remedy to the fitful impulse of a temporary majority of an electorate."

This criticism is really less a criticism of my proposal than a criticism of all popular government. It is wholly unfounded, unless it is founded on the belief that the people are fundamentally untrustworthy. If the Supreme Court's definition of due process in relation to the police power is sound, then an act of the legislature to promote the collective interests of the community must be valid, if it embodies a policy held by the prevailing morality or a preponderant opinion to be necessary to the public welfare.

This is the question that I propose to submit to the people. How can the prevailing morality or a preponderant opinion be better and more exactly ascertained than by a vote of the people? The people must know better than the court what their own morality and their own opinion is. I ask that you, here, you and the others like you, you the people, be given the chance to state your own views of justice and public morality, and not sit meekly by and have your views announced for you by well-meaning adherents of outworn philosophies, who exalt the pedantry of formulas above the vital needs of human life.

The object I have in view could probably be accomplished by an amendment of the State constitutions taking away from the courts the power to review the legislature's determination of a policy of social justice, by defining due process of law in accordance with the views expressed by Justice Holmes of the Supreme Court. But my proposal seems to me more democratic and, I may add, less radical. For under the method I suggest the people may sustain the court as against the legislature, whereas, if due process were defined in the Constitution, the decision of the legislature would be final.

Mr. Taft's position is the position that has been held from the beginning of our government, although not always so openly held, by a large number of reputable and honorable men who, down at bottom, distrust popular government, and, when they must accept it, accept it with reluctance, and hedge it around with every species of restriction and check and balance, so as to make the power of the people as limited and as ineffective as possible.

Mr. Taft fairly defines the issue when he says that our government is and should be a government of all the people by a representative part of the people. This is an excellent and moderate description of an oligarchy. It defines our government as a government of all the people by a few of the people.

Mr. Taft, in his able speech, has made what is probably the best possible presentation of the case for those who feel in this manner. Essentially this view differs only in its expression from the view nakedly set forth by one of his supporters, Congressman Campbell. Congressman Campbell, in a public speech in New Hampshire, in opposing the proposition to give the people real and effective control over all their servants, including the judges, stated that this was equivalent to allowing an appeal from the umpire to the bleachers. Doubtless Congressman Campbell was not himself aware of the cynical truthfulness with which he was putting the real attitude of those for whom he spoke. But it unquestionably is their real attitude. Mr. Campbell's conception of the part the American people should play in self-government is that they should sit on the bleachers and pay the price of admission, but should have nothing to say as to the contest which is waged in the arena by the professional politicians. Apparently Mr. Campbell ignores the fact that the American people are not mere onlookers at a game, that they have a vital stake in the contest, and that democracy means nothing unless they are able and willing to show that they are their own masters.

I am not speaking jokingly, nor do I mean to be unkind; for I repeat that many honorable and well-meaning men of high character take this view, and have taken it from the time of the formation of the nation. Essentially this view is that the Constitution is a straight-jacket to be used for the control of an unruly patient—the people.

Now, I hold that this view is not only false but mischievous, that our constitutions are instruments designed to secure justice by securing the deliberate but effective expression of the popular will, that the checks and balances are valuable as far, and only so far, as they accomplish that deliberation, and that it is a warped and unworthy and improper construction of our form of government to see in it only a means of thwarting the popular will and of preventing justice.

Mr. Taft says that "every class" should have a "voice" in the government. That seems to me a very serious misconception of the American political situation. The real trouble with us is that some classes have had too much voice. One of the most important of all the lessons to be taught and to be learned is that a man should vote, not as a representative of a class, but merely as a good citizen, whose prime interests are the same as those of all other good citizens. The belief in different classes, each having a voice in the government, has given rise to much of our present difficulty; for whosoever believes in these separate classes, each with a voice, inevitably, even although unconsciously, tends to work, not for the good of the whole people, but for the protection of some special class—usually that to which he himself belongs.

The same principle applies when Mr. Taft says that the judiciary ought not to be "representative" of the people in the sense that the legislature and the Executive are. This is perfectly true of the judge when he is performing merely the ordinary functions of a judge in suits between man and man. It is not true of the judge engaged in interpreting, for instance, the due process clause—where the judge is ascertaining the preponderant opinion of the people (as Judge Holmes states it). When he exercises that function he has no right to let his political philosophy reverse and thwart the will of the majority. In that function the judge must represent the people or he fails in the test the Supreme Court has laid down. Take the Workmen's Compensation Act here in New York. The legislators gave us a law in the interest of humanity and decency and fair dealing. In so doing they represented the people, and represented them well. Several judges declared that law constitutional in our State, and several courts in other States declared similar laws constitutional, and the Supreme Court of the nation declared a similar law affecting men in interstate business constitutional; but the highest court in the State of New York, the court of appeals, declared that we, the people of New York, could not have such a law. I hold that in this case the legislators and the judges alike occupied representative positions; the difference was merely that the former represented us well and the latter represented us ill. Remember that the legislators promised that law, and were returned by the people partly in consequence of such promise. That judgment of the people should not have been set aside unless it were irrational. Yet in the Ives case the New York court of appeals praised the policy of the law and the end it sought to obtain; and then declared that the people lacked power to do justice!

Mr. Taft again and again, in quotations I have given and elsewhere through his speech, expresses his disbelief in the people when they vote at the polls. In one sentence he says that the proposition gives "powerful effect to the momentary impulse of a majority of an electorate and prepares the way for the possible exercise of the grossest tyranny." Elsewhere he speaks of the "feverish uncertainty" and "unstable determination" of laws by "temporary and changing majorities"; and again he says that the system I propose "would result in suspension or application of constitutional guaranties according to popular whim," which would destroy "all possible consistency" in constitutional interpretation. I should much like to know the exact distinction that is to be made between what Mr. Taft calls "the fitful impulse of a temporary majority" when applied to a question such as that I raise and any other question. Remember that under my proposal to review a rule of decision by popular vote, amending or construing, to that extent, the Constitution, would certainly take at least two years from the time of the election of the legislature which passed the act. Now, only four months elapse between the nomination and the election of a man as President, to fill for four years the most important office in the land. In one of Mr. Taft's speeches he speaks of "the voice of the people as coming next to the voice of God." Apparently, then, the decision of the people about the presidency, after four months' deliberation, is to be treated as "next to the voice of God"; but if, after two years of sober thought, they decide that women and children shall be protected in industry, or men protected from excessive hours of labor under unhygienic conditions, or wage-workers compensated when they lose life or limb in the service of others, then their decision forthwith becomes a "whim" and "feverish" and "unstable" and an exercise of "the grossest tyranny" and the "laying of the axe to the root of the tree of freedom."

It seems absurd to speak of a conclusion reached by the people after two years' deliberation, after thrashing the matter out before the legislature, after thrashing it out before the governor, after thrashing it out before the court and by the court, and then after full debate for four or six months, as "the fitful impulse of a temporary majority." If Mr. Taft's language correctly describes such action by the people, then he himself and all other Presidents have been elected by "the fitful impulse of a temporary majority"; then the constitution of each State, and the Constitution of the nation, have been adopted, and all amendments thereto have been adopted, by "the fitful impulse of a temporary majority." If he is right, it was "the fitful impulse of a temporary majority" which founded, and another fitful impulse which perpetuated, this nation.

Mr. Taft's position is perfectly clear. It is that we have in this country a special class of persons wiser than the people, who are above the people, who cannot be reached by the people, but who govern them and ought to govern them; and who protect various classes of the people from the whole people. That is the old, old doctrine which has been acted upon for thousands of years abroad; and which here in America has been acted upon sometimes openly, sometimes secretly, for forty years by many men in public and in private life, and I am sorry to say by many judges; a doctrine which has in fact tended to create a bulwark for privilege, a bulwark unjustly protecting special interests against the rights of the people as a whole. This doctrine is to me a dreadful doctrine; for its effect is, and can only be, to make the courts the shield of privilege against popular rights. Naturally, every upholder and beneficiary of crooked privilege loudly applauds the doctrine. It is behind the shield of that doctrine that crooked clauses creep into laws, that men of wealth and power control legislation. The men of wealth who praise this doctrine, this theory, would do well to remember that to its adoption by the courts is due the distrust so many of our wage-workers now feel for the courts. I deny that that theory has worked so well that we should continue it. I most earnestly urge that the evils and abuses it has produced cry aloud for remedy; and the only remedy is in fact to restore the power to govern directly to the people, and to make the public servant directly responsible to the whole people—and to no part of them, to no "class" of them.

Mr. Taft is very much afraid of the tyranny of majorities. For twenty-five years here in New York State, in our efforts to get social and industrial justice, we have suffered from the tyranny of a small minority. We have been denied, now by one court, now by another, as in the Bakeshop Case, where the courts set aside the law limiting the hours of labor in bakeries—the "due process" clause again—as in the Workmen's Compensation Act, as in the Tenement-House Cigar-Factory Case—in all these and many other cases we have been denied by small minorities, by a few worthy men of wrong political philosophy on the bench, the right to protect our people in their lives, their liberty, and their pursuit of happiness. As for "consistency"—why, the record of the courts, in such a case as the income tax, for instance, is so full of inconsistencies as to make the fear expressed of "inconsistency" on the part of the people seem childish.

Well-meaning, short-sighted persons have held up their hands in horror at my proposal to allow the people themselves to construe the constitution which they themselves made. Yet this is precisely what the Association of the Bar of the City of New York proposed to do in the concurrent resolution which was introduced at their request into our legislature on January 16 last, proposing to amend the State constitution by a section reading as follows: "Nothing contained in this Constitution shall be construed to limit the powers of the legislature to enact laws" such as the Workmen's Compensation Act. In other words, the New York Bar Association is proposing to appeal to the people to construe the constitution in such a way as will directly reverse the court. They are proposing to appeal from the highest court of the State to the people. That is just what I propose to do; the difference is only one of method, not of purpose; my method will give better results, and will give them more quickly. The Bar Association by its action admits that the court was wrong, and sets to work to change the rule which it laid down. As Lincoln announced of the Dred Scott decision in his debates with Douglas: "Somebody has to reverse that decision, since it is made, and we mean to reverse it, and we mean to do it peaceably." Was Lincoln wrong? Was the spirit of the nation that wiped out slavery "the fitful impulse of a temporary majority?"

Remember, I am not discussing the recall of judges—although I wish it distinctly understood that the recall is a mere piece of machinery to take the place of the unworkable impeachment which Mr. Taft in effect defends, and that if the days of Maynard ever came back again in the State of New York I should favor it. I have no wish to come to it; but our opponents, when they object to all efforts to secure real justice from the courts, are strengthening the hands of those who demand the recall. In a great many States there has been for many years a real recall of judges as regards appointments, promotions, reappointments, and re-elections; and this recall was through the turn of a thumbscrew at the end of a long-distance rod in the hands of great interests. I believe that a just judge would feel far safer in the hands of the people than in the hands of those interests.

I stand on the Columbus speech. The principles there asserted are not new, but I believe that they are necessary to the maintenance of free democratic government. The part of my speech in which I advocated the right of the people to be the final arbiters of what is due process of law in the case of statutes enacted for the general welfare will ultimately, I am confident, be recognized as giving strength and support to the courts instead of being revolutionary and subversive. The courts to-day owe the country no greater or clearer duty than to keep their hands off such statutes when they have any reasonably permissible relation to the public good. In the past the courts have often failed to perform this duty, and their failure is the chief cause of whatever dissatisfaction there is with the working of our judicial system. One who seeks to prevent the irrevocable commission of such mistakes in the future may justly claim to be regarded as aiming to preserve and not to destroy the independence and power of the judiciary.

My remedy is not the result of a library study of constitutional law, but of actual and long-continued experience in the use of governmental power to redress social and industrial evils. Again and again earnest workers for social justice have said to me that the most serious obstacles that they have encountered during the many years that they have been trying to save American women and children from destruction in American industry have been the courts. That is the judgment of almost all the social workers I know, and of dozens of parish priests and clergymen, and of every executive and legislator who has been seriously attempting to use government as an agency for social and industrial betterment. What is the result of this system of judicial nullification? It was accurately stated by the court of appeals of New York in the employers' liability case, where it was calmly and judicially declared that the people under our Republican government are less free to correct the evils that oppress them than are the people of the monarchies of Europe.

To any man with vision, to any man with broad and real social sympathies, to any man who believes with all his heart in this great democratic Republic of ours, such a condition is intolerable. It is not government by the people, but mere sham government in which the will of the people is constantly defeated. It is out of this experience that my remedy has come; and let it be tried in this field. When, as the result of years of education and debate, a majority of the people have decided upon a remedy for an evil from which they suffer, and have chosen a legislature and executive pledged to embody that remedy in law, and the law has been finally passed and approved, I regard it as monstrous that a bench of judges shall then say to the people: "You must begin all over again. First amend your Constitution (which will take four years); second, secure the passage of a new law (which will take two years more); third, carry that new law over the weary course of litigation (which will take no human being knows how long); fourth, submit the whole matter over again to the very same judges who have rendered the decision to which you object. Then, if your patience holds out and you finally prevail, the will of the majority of the people may have its way."

Such a system is not popular government, but a mere mockery of popular government. It is a system framed to maintain and perpetuate social injustice, and it can be defended only by those who disbelieve in the people, who do not trust them, and, I am afraid I must add, who have no real and living sympathy with them as they struggle for better things.

In lieu of it I propose a practice by which the will of a majority of the people, when they have determined upon a remedy, shall, if their will persists for a minimum period of two years, go straight forward until it becomes a ruling force of life. I expressly propose to provide that sufficient time be taken to make sure that the remedy expresses the will, the sober and well-thought-out judgment, and not the whim, of the people; but, when that has been ascertained, I am not willing that the will of the people shall be frustrated. If this be not a wise remedy, let those who criticise it propose a wise remedy, and not confine themselves to railing at government by a majority of the American people as government by the mob. To propose, as an alternative remedy, slight modifications of impeachment proceedings is to propose no remedy at all—it is to bid us to be content with chaff when we demand bread.

The decisions of which we complain are, as a rule, based upon the constitutional provision that no person shall be deprived of life, liberty, or property without due process of law. The terms "life, liberty, and property" have been used in the constitutions of the English-speaking peoples since Magna Carta. Until within the last sixty years they were treated as having specific meanings; "property" meant tangible property; "liberty" meant freedom from personal restraint, or, in other words, from imprisonment in its largest definition. About 1870 our courts began to attach to these terms new meanings. Now "property" has come to mean every right of value which a person could enjoy, and "liberty" has been made to include the right to make contracts. As a result, when the State limits the hours for which women may labor, it is told by the courts that this law deprives them of their "liberty"; and when it restricts the manufacture of tobacco in a tenement, it is told that the law deprives the landlord of his "property." Now, I do not believe that any people, and especially our free American people, will long consent that the term "liberty" shall be defined for them by a bench of judges. Every people has defined that term for itself in the course of its historic development. Of course, it is plain enough to see that, in a large way, the political history of man may be grouped about these three terms, "life, liberty, and property." There is no act of government which cannot be brought within their definition, and if the courts are to cease to treat them as words having a limited, specific meaning, then our whole government is brought under the practically irresponsible supervision of judges. As against that kind of a government I insist that the people have the right, and can be trusted, to govern themselves. This our opponents deny; and the issue is sharply drawn between us.

If my critics would only show the same sober judgment of which they declare the people at large to be incapable, they would realize that my proposal is one of moderation and common sense. I wish to quote the remarks of William Draper Lewis, dean of the Law School of the University of Pennsylvania:

"To a lawyer the most interesting suggestion Colonel Roosevelt has made is to allow the people, after consideration, to re-enact legislation which a court decision has declared is contrary to some clause in the existing State constitution.

"Any one who has been asked to draft specific amendments to State constitutions will hesitate to condemn, without serious consideration, the suggestion made by Colonel Roosevelt. To take a concrete instance: The New York court of appeals declared the Workmen's Compensation Act, passed by the New York legislature, unconstitutional, as depriving in its operation the employer of his property without due process of law. A number of amendments to the New York constitution, designed to validate a compensation act, have been drafted, and it is not unlikely that one of them will be adopted. Personally, one or more of these amendments having been shown to me, I cannot but feel that constitutional amendments, designed to meet particular cases, run the danger of being so worded as to produce far-reaching results not anticipated or desired by the people. Colonel Roosevelt's suggestion avoids this difficulty and danger. If a persistent majority of the people of New York State want a workmen's compensation act, they should have it. But, in order to obtain it, they should not be driven to pass an amendment to their State constitution which may have effects which they do not anticipate or desire. Let them pass on the act, as passed by the legislature, after a full knowledge that their highest court has unanimously expressed its opinion that the act is contrary to the State constitution which the people at a prior election have declared to be their fundamental law.

"I may not always approve of what the persistent majority wants. I might sometimes think the measure unwise. But that doesn't alter the right of that majority to enforce its will in government. The Roosevelt idea, it seems to me, supplies an instrument by which that majority can enforce its will in the most conservative way. It makes explosions unnecessary.

"I would have been very proud to have been the author of that plan, although I want to emphasize the fact that it involves no new principle, only a new method.

"I don't mind saying, however, that I think it unfortunate that it should have been proposed by Colonel Roosevelt. He is a man of such marked characteristics, and his place in the political world is such, that he arouses intense enthusiasm on the one hand, and intense animosity on the other. Because of this, the great idea which he has propounded is bound to be beclouded, and its adoption to be delayed. It is a pity that anything so important should be confounded with any man's personality."

As regards the dean's last paragraph, I can only say that I wish somebody else whose suggestions would arouse less antagonism had proposed it; but nobody else did propose it, and so I had to. I am not leading this fight as a matter of aesthetic pleasure. I am leading because somebody must lead, or else the fight would not be made at all.

I prefer to work with moderate, with rational, conservatives, provided only that they do in good faith strive forward toward the light. But when they halt and turn their backs to the light, and sit with the scorners on the seats of reaction, then I must part company with them. We the people cannot turn back. Our aim must be steady, wise progress. It would be well if our people would study the history of a sister republic. All the woes of France for a century and a quarter have been due to the folly of her people in splitting into the two camps of unreasonable conservatism and unreasonable radicalism. Had pre-Revolutionary France listened to men like Turgot, and backed them up, all would have gone well. But the beneficiaries of privilege, the Bourbon reactionaries, the short-sighted ultra-conservatives, turned down Turgot; and then found that instead of him they had obtained Robespierre. They gained twenty years' freedom from all restraint and reform, at the cost of the whirlwind of the red terror; and in their turn the unbridled extremists of the terror induced a blind reaction; and so, with convulsion and oscillation from one extreme to another, with alternations of violent radicalism and violent Bourbonism, the French people went through misery toward a shattered goal. May we profit by the experiences of our brother republicans across the water, and go forward steadily, avoiding all wild extremes; and may our ultra-conservatives remember that the rule of the Bourbons brought on the Revolution, and may our would-be revolutionaries remember that no Bourbon was ever such a dangerous enemy of the people and of freedom as the professed friend of both, Robespierre. There is no danger of a revolution in this country; but there is grave discontent and unrest, and in order to remove them there is need of all the wisdom and probity and deep-seated faith in and purpose to uplift humanity we have at our command.

Friends, our task as Americans is to strive for social and industrial justice, achieved through the genuine rule of the people. This is our end, our purpose. The methods for achieving the end are merely expedients, to be finally accepted or rejected according as actual experience shows that they work well or ill. But in our hearts we must have this lofty purpose, and we must strive for it in all earnestness and sincerity, or our work will come to nothing. In order to succeed we need leaders of inspired idealism, leaders to whom are granted great visions, who dream greatly and strive to make their dreams come true; who can kindle the people with the fire from their own burning souls. The leader for the time being, whoever he may be, is but an instrument, to be used until broken and then to be cast aside; and if he is worth his salt he will care no more when he is broken than a soldier cares when he is sent where his life is forfeit in order that the victory may be won. In the long fight for righteousness the watchword for all of us is spend and be spent. It is of little matter whether any one man fails or succeeds; but the cause shall not fail, for it is the cause of mankind.

We, here in America, hold in our hands the hope of the world, the fate of the coming years; and shame and disgrace will be ours if in our eyes the light of high resolve is dimmed, if we trail in the dust the golden hopes of men. If on this new continent we merely build another country of great but unjustly divided material prosperity, we shall have done nothing; and we shall do as little if we merely set the greed of envy against the greed of arrogance, and thereby destroy the material well-being of all of us. To turn this government either into government by a plutocracy or government by a mob would be to repeat on a larger scale the lamentable failures of the world that is dead. We stand against all tyranny, by the few or by the many. We stand for the rule of the many in the interest of all of us, for the rule of the many in a spirit of courage, of common sense, of high purpose, above all in a spirit of kindly justice toward every man and every woman. We not merely admit, but insist, that there must be self-control on the part of the people, that they must keenly perceive their own duties as well as the rights of others; but we also insist that the people can do nothing unless they not merely have, but exercise to the full, their own rights. The worth of our great experiment depends upon its being in good faith an experiment—the first that has ever been tried—in true democracy on the scale of a continent, on a scale as vast as that of the mightiest empires of the Old World. Surely this is a noble ideal, an ideal for which it is worth while to strive, an ideal for which at need it is worth while to sacrifice much; for our ideal is the rule of all the people in a spirit of friendliest brotherhood toward each and every one of the people.

The Recall of Judicial Decisions

In the New York *World* of Thursday appears a detailed statement that some very eminent lawyers of New York have undertaken the formation of what they style the

Address at Philadelphia, Pennsylvania, April 10, 1912; in Progressive Principles (Works, vol. 17)

"Independent Judiciary Association." They propose, to use their own words, "to combat the spread of two ideas," namely, the recall of judges, and the referendum to the people of a certain class of cases of judicial decisions; and they assert, in President Taft's words, that these ideas "lay the axe at the root of the tree of well-ordered freedom." Many of the signers are distinguished men, standing high in their community; but we can gain a clew as to just what kind of well-ordered freedom they have in mind, the kind of "freedom" to the defense of which they are rushing, when we see among the signers of this call the names of attorneys for a number of corporations not distinguished for a high-keyed sense of civic duty, or for their disinterested conduct toward the public. . . . The head of the association is announced to be Mr. Choate; and one of the members is Mr. Milburn, who in 1904 was the head of the Parker Constitution Club, a similar body, with a similar purpose, namely, to uphold privilege and sustain the special interests against the cause of justice and against the interest of the people as a whole.

I hold absolutely to my conviction that some basis of accommodation must be found between the declared policy of the States on matters of social justice within the proper scope of regulation in the interest of health, of decent living and working conditions, and of morals, and the attempt of the courts to substitute their own ideas on these subjects for the declarations of the people, made through their elected representatives in the several States. . . .

I do not question the good purposes of some of these gentlemen. But they are intelligent men, trained in their profession; and some of them must have at least a smattering of knowledge of the constitutions of our own and other countries. On the assumption that they have both intelligence and knowledge, it is impossible to credit them with good faith in the fears that they have expressed as above quoted; except on the supposition that their long experience as attorneys for corporations has finally rendered them genuinely unable to understand justice, and genuinely unable to think of a judge except as an instrument devised to protect privilege against the rights of the people by invoking the technicalities of the law for the purpose of preventing the obtaining of justice under the law. This is a strong statement; and I would not make it of ordinary men who are misled by reading those New York papers owned or controlled by Wall Street and who are misled by their belief in Mr. Choate and Mr. Milburn. As regards those citizens I have nothing to say except that I wish it were possible for them to have access to channels of information which were not wilfully poisoned. But with Messrs. Choate and Milburn and their associates the case is wholly different. These men are not to be excused on the plea of ignorance.

My proposal is for the exercise of the referendum by the people themselves in a certain class of decisions of constitutional questions in which the courts decide against the power of the people to do elementary justice. When men of trained intelligence call this "putting the axe to the tree of well-ordered freedom," it is quite impossible to reconcile their statements both with good faith and with even reasonably full knowledge of the facts.

All that is necessary to do in order to prove the absolute correctness of the statement I have just made is to call your attention to the plain and obvious facts in the case. In the first place, consider the present practice in various countries in which there is substantially the same well-ordered freedom as in our own land. For instance, take the republic of France and the great English-speaking commonwealths of the British Empire, England, Canada, Australia, all of which are governed by the Parliaments in substantially the same manner that we are governed. In every country I have named the decision of the legislature on constitutional questions is absolute and not subject to action by the judiciary; and whenever the courts make a decision which the legislature regards as establishing a construction of the constitution which is unwarranted, the legislature, if it chooses, can by law override that construction and establish its own construction of the constitution. . . .

Now, Mr. Milburn is by birth an Englishman, and Mr. Choate has been ambassador to England, and it is quite impossible that they can be sincere in asserting that "well-ordered freedom" would be destroyed in this country by adopting a practice by no means as extreme (from the standpoint of giving the people instead of the courts the ultimate power to decide certain constitutional questions) as the practice which now obtains, and which always has obtained in England, in France since it was a republic, and just across our own border in Canada and in every province of Canada.

Either Messrs. Choate and Milburn hold that there is no "well-ordered freedom" in England, Scotland, in Australia, in Ontario, New Brunswick, or Manitoba, which is preposterous, or else they must admit that they are talking nonsense when they say that the adoption of my proposal would mean the destruction of "well-ordered freedom" in this country. . . .

Now, consider my proposal itself; and I shall illustrate it by two or three concrete cases which will show just what the attitude of these great corporation lawyers is on questions of fundamental justice as against special privilege. My proposal is merely to secure to the people the right which the Supreme Court, speaking through Mr. Justice Holmes, in the Oklahoma Bank Cases, say they undoubtedly should possess. My proposal is that the people shall have the power to decide for themselves, in the last resort, what legislation is necessary in exercising the police powers, the general welfare powers, so as to give expression to the general morality, the general opinion, of the people. In England, Canada, and the other countries I have mentioned, no one dreams that the court has a right to express an opinion in such matters as against the will of the people shown by the action of the legislature. I do not propose to go as far as this. I do not propose to do in these matters what England, Canada, Australia, and France have always done, that is, make the legislature supreme over the courts in these cases. I merely propose to make legislature and court alike responsible to the sober and deliberate judgment of the people, who are masters of both legislature and courts.

... I am not dealing with any case of justice as between man and man, nor am I speaking of the Federal courts, which, because of the peculiar features of our Constitution, must be treated by themselves. Nor am I speaking of the recall of judges. ... I am seeking to introduce a system which will obviate the need of such a drastic measure as the recall. If in any case the legislature has passed a law under the police power for the purpose of promoting social and industrial justice and the courts declare it in conflict with the fundamental law of the State, the constitution as laid down by the people, then I propose that after due deliberation—for a period which could not be for less than two years after the passage of the original law—the people shall themselves have the right to declare whether or not the proposed law is to be treated as constitutional.

It is a matter of mere terminology whether this is called a method of construing or applying the Constitution, or a quicker method of getting the Constitution amended. It is certainly far superior to the ordinary method of getting the Constitution amended, because it will apply merely to the case at issue, and therefore would be definite and clear in its action; whereas, actual experience with the Fourteenth

Amendment to the National Constitution, for instance, has shown us that an amendment passed by the people with one purpose may be given by the courts a construction which makes it apply to wholly different purposes and in a wholly different manner. The Fourteenth Amendment has been construed by the courts to apply to a multitude of cases to which it is positive the people who passed the amendment had not the remotest idea of applying it.

Some of my opponents say that under my proposal there would be conflicting interpretations by the people of the Constitution. In the first place, this is mere guesswork on the part of our opponents. In the next place, the people could not decide in more conflicting fashion, could not possibly make their decisions conflict with one another to a greater degree, than has actually been the case with the courts. No popular vote could reverse an earlier popular vote more completely than was the case with the decisions of the Supreme Court in the Legal Tender Cases and the Income Tax Cases. At this moment the courts of Massachusetts, Iowa, and Washington, and the Supreme Court of the nation, construe clauses of the Constitution to permit one thing and the court of appeals in New York construes identically the same language to mean the direct reverse, and this not as regards unimportant matters, but as regards matters of vital importance to the welfare of hundreds of thousands of citizens, in cases like the Workmen's Compensation Act and the act limiting the hours of labor for women in factories.

The best way to test the merits of my proposal is to consider a few specimen cases to which it would apply. Within the last thirty years the court of appeals of New York has been one of the most formidable obstacles to social reform, one of the most formidable obstacles in the way of getting industrial justice, which men who strive for justice have had to encounter. Among very many other laws which this court has made abortive, or decided not to be laws on the ground that they conflicted with the Constitution, are the following:

(1) The law for preventing the manufacture of tobacco in tenement-houses; the decision of the court in this case retarded by at least twenty years the work of tenement-house reform, and was directly responsible for causing hundreds of thousands of American citizens now alive to be brought up under conditions of reeking filth and squalor, which immeasurably decreased their chance of turning out to be good citizens. Yet this decision was rendered by perfectly well-meaning men who knew law, but who did not know life, and who, forsooth, based their decision on the ground that they would not permit legislation to interfere with the "sanctity of the home"—the home in question in many cases having precisely the "sanctity" that attaches to one room in which two large families, one with a boarder, live and work day and night, the tobacco they manufacture being surrounded with every kind of filth.

(2) The courts held unconstitutional the law under which a girl was endeavoring to recover damages for the loss of her arm, taken off because dangerous machinery was not guarded. In this case the judges announced that they were "protecting the girl's liberty" to work where she would endanger life and limb if she chose! Of course, as the girl had no liberty save the "liberty" of starving or else of working under the dangerous conditions, the courts were merely protecting the liberty of her employer to endanger the lives of his employees, or kill or cripple them, with immunity to himself. I do not believe that in our entire history there is an instance in which a majority of the voters have showed such tyranny and such callous indifference to the suffering of a minority as were shown by these doubtless well-meaning judges in this case.

(3) When the legislature of New York passed a law limit-

ing the hours of labor of women in factories to ten hours a day for six days a week, and forbade their being employed after nine in the evening and before six in the morning, the New York court of appeals declared it unconstitutional, and a malign inspiration induced them to state in their opinion that the time had come for courts "fearlessly" to interpose a barrier against such legislation. Fearlessly! The court fearlessly condemned helpless women to be worked at inhuman toil for hours so long as to make it impossible that they should retain health or strength; and "fearlessly" upheld the right of big factory owners and small sweat-shop owners to coin money out of the blood of the wretched women and girls whom they worked haggard for their own profit. To protect such wrongdoers was of course an outrage upon the decent and high-minded factory owners who did not wish to work the women and girls to an excessive degree, but who were forced to do so by the competition of the callous factory owners whom the court, by this decision, deliberately aided and abetted in their wrong-doing. Court after court in other States, including as conservative a State as Massachusetts, have declared such a law as this constitutional, yet the court of appeals in New York declared it unconstitutional. No popular majority vote could ever be more inconsistent with another popular majority vote than is the record of the court of appeals of New York in this matter when compared with the record of other courts in other States.

(4) The Workmen's Compensation Act, but a year or two ago, was declared unconstitutional by the court of appeals of New York, although a directly reverse decision in precisely similar language had been rendered not only by the State courts of Iowa and Washington, but by the Supreme Court of the United States. Here again it is worth while to point out that no vote by popular majority could render the Constitution more uncertain of construction than the court

of appeals of New York rendered it by making the decision it did in the teeth of the decision of the Supreme Court and of other State courts; and throughout our history no decision by a majority of the people in any State has shown more flagrant disregard of the elementary rights of a minority, no popular vote has ever in any State more flagrantly denied justice, than was the case in this decision by the highest court of the State of New York, but a year or two ago.

Now, in these cases in New York under the plan I propose, the people of the State of New York, after due deliberation, would have had an opportunity to decide for themselves whether the constitution which they themselves made should or should not be so construed as to prevent them from doing elementary justice in these matters. Remember also that in this case the conflict was not only between the New York legislature and the New York court. The New York court also took square issue, in its construction of constitutional provisions, with the position taken by State courts elsewhere in the Union, and with the position taken by the Supreme Court of the United States.

It would be an absolute physical impossibility for the people of the State, voting at the polls, to have interpreted the constitution more mischievously than the court of appeals has repeatedly interpreted it during the last quarter of a century, as regards the class of cases which I am now considering.

My proposal is merely to give the people an effective constitutional weapon for use against wrong and injustice. Messrs. Choate and Milburn and their allies, in taking the position they do, nakedly champion vested wrong. They appear as the champions and apologists of privilege as against the mass of our people—the farmers, the working men, the small shopkeeper, the decent hard-working citizens of every grade. They defend the courts because the courts in these cases I have mentioned have done injustice, have decided against the people, have decided in favor of the special interests and in favor of privilege. I do not question the good intentions of most of the great lawyers who take this attitude. But the only alternative to questioning their good intentions is to admit that their life-long association with corporations, the habits they have contracted by acting as highly paid special pleaders for privilege, for special interests and for vested wrong, and their utter ignorance of real life and of the needs of the people as a whole, have rendered them unfit to act as advisers of the public, unfit to know what justice is.

Messrs. Choate and Milburn and their associates in effect take the position that the people have not the right to secure workmen's compensation laws, or laws limiting the hours of labor for women in factories, or laws protecting workers from dangerous machinery, or laws making conditions decent in tenement-houses. It is a mere sham for any man to say that he approves of such laws so long as he upholds the courts in declaring them unconstitutional, so long as he fails to approve thoroughgoing action which will give the people power, with reasonable speed, to upset such court decision and to secure real and substantial justice. Messrs. Choate and Milburn say that we are "putting the axe to the root of the tree of well-ordered freedom," when we ask that New York—and every other State where there is need—take effective steps to provide such legislation as many other States of the Union already possess, and as almost every other civilized country outside of the United States has on the statute-books. A more absurd pleas was never made than this plea that "well-ordered freedom" will be destroyed by doing justice to men, women, and children who are ground down by excessive toil under conditions ruinous to life and limb; and this, and precisely this, and nothing but this, is what our opponents say when their statement is stripped of verbiage. In this matter Messrs. Choate and Milburn and their associates appear as the attorneys of privilege, as special pleaders for special interests, and as the representatives of those great corporations that deny justice to small competitors and to their employees and their customers; and they appear against the people as a whole, and are hostile to the essentials of justice.

Vermont is a State in which "well-ordered freedom" certainly obtains. Are Messrs. Choate and Milburn aware that in Vermont the actual practice about the judges is that they are appointed practically for life, but subject to recall, and therefore to a referendum on their actions, every two years? In that State the judges are elected by the legislature, and in practice the legislature always re-elects the judge as long as he wishes to serve, unless he proves unfaithful, when the principle of the recall is applied by the simple process of not re-electing him. In the last twenty or thirty years this has been done in but one case. In Vermont the judges are as upright and independent as any judges in the Union; but in constitutional cases such as those I have mentioned they do really represent, and not misrepresent, the people.

In short, Messrs. Choate and Milburn and their associates, if their language is to be accepted as sincere, know nothing of the position taken by courts and legislatures in other lands as regards these constitutional questions, know little as to what has been done in certain of our own States thereon, and know practically nothing about the needs of the immense bulk of their countrymen. They do not even know what is elementary knowledge among the men specially trained in constitutional law in their country; men like Dean Lewis, of the University of Pennsylvania Law School, and Professor Scofield, professor of law at the Northwestern Law School. In a recent article Professor Scofield has shown that the State courts of Illinois have behaved no better than the State courts of New York in these matters. He quotes the emphatic criticisms of these decisions of which I complain by the late Dean Thayer, of the Harvard Law School. He says that these decisions make of the law a weapon with which the strong can strike down the weak, that they make of the law not a shield to protect the people, but a sword to smite down the people; that they are arbitrary, and that our protest against them represents one phase of the struggle against arbitrary power and in favor of the law of the land, and he sees that my proposal is merely to use a constitutional method to restore to the State law-making bodies the power which the Supreme Court of this nation says belongs to them.

There are sincere and well-meaning men of timid nature who are frightened by the talk of tyranny of the majority. Those worthy gentlemen are nearly a century behind the times. It is true that De Tocqueville, writing about eighty years ago, said that in this country there was great tyranny by the majority. His statement may have been true then, although certainly not to the degree he insisted, but it is not true now. That profound and keen thinker, Mr. James Bryce, in "The American Commonwealth" treats of this in his chapter on the "Tyranny of the Majority" by saying that it does not exist. His own words are that:

"It is no longer a blemish on the American system, and the charges against democracy from the supposed example of America are groundless. The fact that the danger once dreaded has now disappeared is no small evidence of the recuperative forces of the American Government, and the healthy tone of the American people."

I wish that our opponents, Mr. Taft, Mr. Choate, Mr. Milburn, Mr. Penrose, Mr. Guggenheim, Mr. Lorimer, and the rest of their companions, who so dread and distrust the American people, would in this matter copy the good faith and sanity of the learned and able ambassador from Great Britain.

I shall protest against the tyranny of the majority whenever it arises, just as I shall protest against every other form of tyranny. But at present we are not suffering in any way from the tyranny of the majority. We suffer from the tyranny of the bosses and of the special interests, that is, from the tyranny of minorities. Mr. Choate, Mr. Milburn, and their allies are acting as the servants and spokesmen of the special interests and are standing cheek by jowl with the worst representatives of politics when they seek to keep the courts in the grasp of privilege and of the politicians; for this is all they accomplish when they prevent them from being responsible in proper fashion to the people. These worthy gentlemen speak as if the judges were somehow imposed on us by Heaven, and were responsible only to Heaven. As a matter of fact judges are human just like other people, and in this country they will either be chosen by the people and responsible to the people, or they will be chosen by, and responsible to, the bosses and the special interests and the political and financial beneficiaries of privilege. It is this last system which Mr. Choate and Mr. Milburn and their allies are by their actions upholding. In the course they are taking, they and the respectable men associated with them, are, in some cases certainly unconsciously, and in other cases I fear consciously, acting on behalf of the special interests, political and financial, and in favor of privilege, and against the interest of the plain people and against the cause of justice and of human right. In the long run this country will not be a good place for any of us to live in unless it is a reasonably good place for all of us to live in; and it will neither become nor remain a good place for all of us to live in if we permit our government to be turned aside from its original purpose and to become a government such as Mr. Taft, Mr. Choate, Mr. Lorimer, Mr. Milburn, Mr. Penrose, Mr. Guggenheim, and their allies wish to make it—a government by corporation attorneys on the bench and off the bench; and this without regard to whether particular individuals among these corporation attorneys mean well or mean ill, without regard to whether they are or are not conscious of the fact that they are really serving the cause of special privilege and not the cause of the people.

Limitation of Governmental Power

In one of his campaign speeches Mr. Wilson made a sweeping assault on the Progressive platform and programme and defined his own position as to social and industrial justice. According to the stenographic report of his speech, Mr. Wilson stated that there is no hope for social reform through the platform of the Progressive party, saying: "In the very form itself is supplied the demonstration that it is not a serviceable instrument. They do propose to serve civilization and humanity but they cannot serve civilization and humanity with that kind of government. . . . The history of liberty is a history of the limitation of governmental power, not the increase of it."

And he then continues to uphold what he calls "representative" government and "representative" assemblies as against the platform that we propose, and also to uphold the Democratic proposals for dealing with labor and the trusts as against the Progressive proposals.

Mr. Wilson is fond of asserting his platonic devotion to the purposes of the Progressive party. But such platonic devotion is utterly worthless from a practical standpoint, because he antagonizes the only means by which those purposes can be made effective. It is idle to profess devotion to Progressive principles and at the same time to antagonize the only methods by which they can be realized in actual fact.

Address at the Coliseum, San Francisco, September 14, 1912; in Progressive Principles (Works, vol. 17)

The key to Mr. Wilson's position is found in the statement I have just quoted, when he says that "The history of liberty is a history of the limitation of governmental power, not the increase of it."

This is a bit of outworn academic doctrine which was kept in the schoolroom and the professorial study for a generation after it had been abandoned by all who had experience of actual life. It is simply the *laissez-faire* doctrine of the English political economists three-quarters of a century ago. It can be applied with profit, if anywhere at all, only in a primitive community under primitive conditions, in a community such as the United States at the end of the eighteenth century, a community before the days of Fulton, Morse and Edison. To apply it now in the United States at the beginning of the twentieth century, with its highly organized industries, with its railways, telegraphs, and telephones, means literally and absolutely to refuse to make a single effort to better any one of our social or industrial conditions.

Moreover, Mr. Wilson is absolutely in error in his statement, from the historical standpoint.

So long as governmental power existed exclusively for the king and not at all for the people, then the history of liberty was a history of the limitation of governmental power. But now the governmental power rests in the people, and the kings who enjoy privilege are the kings of the financial and industrial world; and what they clamor for is the limitation of governmental power, and what the people sorely need is the extension of governmental power.

If Mr. Wilson's statement means nothing, then he ought not to have made it.

If it means anything, it means that every law for the promotion of social and industrial justice which has been put upon the statute-books ought to be repealed, and every law proposed should be abandoned, for without exception every such law represents an increase of governmental power. Does Mr. Wilson mean to repeal the interstate commerce commission law? If not, does he deny that it represents a great increase of governmental power over the railroads? Let him take whichever horn of the dilemma he chooses. Either his statement is not in accordance with the facts or else he is bound, if it is in accordance with the facts as he sees them, to include in his programme the repeal of the Interstate Commerce Commission Act.

Again, every Progressive State in the Union has passed laws for factory inspection; every such law means an increase of governmental power. Is Mr. Wilson in favor of repealing those laws? If he is not, then what does he mean by saying that the history of liberty is the history of the limitation of governmental power?

The fact is that this statement is a mere bit of professorial rhetoric, which has not one particle of foundation in the facts of the present day.

Again, we propose to limit the hours of working girls to eight hours a day; we propose to limit the hours of working men in continuous industries to eight hours a day, and to give them one day's rest a week. Both of these proposals represent an increase in the exercise of governmental power, an extension of governmental power. Does Mr. Wilson mean that he is against this extension? If not, then his sentence which I have just quoted and which represents the key-note of his speech, means nothing whatever.

In other words, Mr. Wilson's promise is either a promise that is not to be kept or else it means the undoing of every particle of social and industrial advance we have made and the refusal to go forward along the lines of industrial and social progress.

He stands for a policy which necessarily means, if that policy is honestly put into effect, that he must be against every single progressive measure, for every progressive mea-

sure means an extension, instead of a limitation, of governmental control.

We propose to do away with occupational disease. Is he
against this proposition? He must be if he believes in limitation of governmental control.

We propose a workman's compensation act. Is he against
this proposition? He must be if he sincerely means that he is
in favor of the limitation of governmental control.

We propose to regulate the conditions of work in factories, the conditions of life in tenement-houses, the conditions of life and work in construction camps—every one of
these proposals means an extension of governmental control. Is he against them?

Either he is against his own principle or he is against
these reforms. He can choose either horn of the dilemma he
wishes; but one or the other he must choose.

He has definitely committed himself to the use of the tax-
ing power only for the purpose of raising revenue. In that
case he is against its use to put out of existence the poisonous-
match industry. He is against its use for the purpose of preventing opium coming into this country. He is against its
use for preventing wildcat banking. In short, he is against
its use in every case where we now use it to tax out of existence dangers and abuses.

The trouble with Mr. Wilson is that he is following an
outworn philosophy and that the history of which he is
thinking is the history of absolute monarchies and Oriental
despotisms. He is thinking of government as embodied in
an absolute king or in an oligarchy or aristocracy. He is not
thinking of our government, which is a government by the
people themselves.

The only way in which our people can increase their
power over the big corporation that does wrong, the only
way in which they can protect the working man in his conditions of work and life, the only way in which the people

can prevent children working in industry or secure women an eight-hour day in industry, or secure compensation for men killed or crippled in industry, is by extending, instead of limiting, the powers of government.

There is no analogy whatever from the standpoint of real liberty, and of real popular need, between the limitations imposed by the people on the power of an irresponsible monarch or a dominant aristocracy, and the limitation sought to be imposed by big financiers, by big corporation lawyers, and by well-meaning students of a dead-and-gone system of political economy on the power of the people to right social wrongs and limit social abuses, and to secure for the humble what, unless there is an extension of the powers of government, the arrogant and the powerful will certainly take from the humble.

If Mr. Wilson really believes what he has said, then Mr. Wilson has no idea of our government in its actual working. He is not thinking of modern American history or of present-day American needs. He is thinking of *Magna Carta*, which limited the power of the English king, because his power over the people had before been absolute. He is thinking of the Bill of Rights, which limited the power of the governing class in the interest of the people, who could not control that governing class.

Our proposal is to increase the power of the people themselves and to make the people in reality the governing class. Therefore Mr. Wilson's proposal is really to limit the power of the people and thereby to leave unchecked the colossal embodied privileges of the present day.

Now, you can adopt one philosophy or the other. You can adopt the philosophy of *laissez-faire*, of the limitation of governmental power, and turn the industrial life of this country into a chaotic scramble of selfish interests, each bent on plundering the other and all bent on oppressing the wage-worker. This is precisely and exactly what Mr. Wilson's proposal means; and it can mean nothing else. Under such limitations of governmental power as he praises, every railroad must be left unchecked, every great industrial concern can do as it chooses with its employees and with the general public; women must be permitted to work as many hours a day as their taskmasters bid them; great corporations must be left unshackled to put down wages to a starvation limit and to raise the price of their products as high as monopolistic control will permit.

The reverse policy means an extension, instead of a limitation, of governmental power; and for that extension, we Progressives stand.

We propose to handle the colossal industrial concerns engaged in interstate business as we are handling the great railways engaged in interstate business; and we propose to go forward in the control of both, doing justice to each but exacting justice from each; and we propose to work for justice to the farmer and the wage-worker in the same fashion.

Let me give you a concrete instance of what Mr. Wilson's policy . . .

The people of the United States have but one instrument which they can efficiently use against the colossal combinations of business—and that instrument is the government of the United States (and of course in the several States the governments of the States where they can be utilized). Mr. Wilson's proposal is that the people of the United States shall throw away this, the one great instrument, the one great weapon they have with which to secure themselves against wrong. He proposes to limit the governmental action of the people and therefore to leave unlimited and unchecked the action of the great corporations whose enormous power constitutes so serious a problem in modern industrial life. Remember that it is absolutely impossible to limit the power of these great corporations whose enormous power constitutes so serious a problem in modern industrial life except by extending the power of the government. All that these great corporations ask is that the power of the government shall be limited. No wonder they are supporting Mr. Wilson, for he is advocating for them what they hardly dare venture to advocate for themselves. These great corporations rarely want anything from the government except to be let alone and to be permitted to work their will unchecked by the government. All that they really want is that governmental action shall be limited. In every great corporation suit the corporation lawyer will be found protesting against extension of governmental power. Every court decision favoring a corporation takes the form of declaring unconstitutional some extension of governmental power. Every corporation magnate in the country who is not dealing honestly and fairly by his fellows asks nothing better than that Mr. Wilson's programme he carried out and that there be stringent limitations of governmental power.

There once was a time in history when the limitation of governmental power meant increasing liberty for the people. In the present day the limitation of governmental power, of governmental action, means the enslavement of the people by the great corporations who can only be held in check through the extension of governmental power.

In another speech Mr. Wilson has taken his stand squarely on the Democratic platform about the tariff. The Democratic platform says the tariff is unconstitutional. . . . Mr. Wilson states that the protective tariff is "a malignant growth that requires a surgical operation." . . . If a protective tariff is unconstitutional, if a protective tariff is "a malignant growth" which he proposes to "cut out," then it is disingenuous to say that the operation shall be done in slow and leisurely fashion so as not to damage the patient. A malignant growth must be cut out at once; an unconstitutional law must be repealed at once.

The Republican proposal is a tariff for privilege; the

Democratic proposal is a tariff for destruction; the Progressive proposal is a tariff for labor, a tariff which shall give to the American business man his fair [share], both permitting and requiring him to pay the American laborer the wages necessary to keep up the standard of living in this country.

Mr. Wilson's attitude toward the tariff is exactly in keeping with his attitude toward social and industrial reforms. He is against the minimum wage for women exactly as he is against a protective tariff. His principles would prevent us either effectually helping labor or effectually regulating and controlling big business.

He is against using the power of the government to help the people to whom the government belongs.

We take flat issue with him. We propose to use the government as the most efficient instrument for the uplift of our people as a whole; we propose to give a fair chance to the workers and strengthen their rights. We propose to use the whole power of the government to protect all those who, under Mr. Wilson's *laissez-faire* system, are trodden down in the ferocious, scrambling rush of an unregulated and purely individualistic industrialism.

How I Became a Progressive

I suppose I had a natural tendency to become a Progressive, anyhow. That is, I was naturally a democrat in believing in fair play for everybody. But I grew toward my present position, not so much as the result of study in the library or the reading of books—although I have been very much helped by such study and by such reading—as by actually living and working with men under many different conditions and seeing their needs from many different points of view.

The first set of our people with whom I associated so inti-

The Outlook, October 12, 1912; in Social Justice and Popular Rule (Works, vol. 17)

mately as to get on thoroughly sympathetic terms with them were cow-punchers, then on the ranges in the West. I was so impressed with them that in doing them justice I did injustice to equally good citizens elsewhere whom I did not know; and it was a number of years before I grew to understand, first by associating with railway men, then with farmers, then with mechanics, and so on, that the things that I specially liked about my cow-puncher friends were, after all, to be found fundamentally in railway men, in farmers, in blacksmiths, in carpenters—in fact, generally among my fellow American citizens.

Before I began to go with the cow-punchers, I had already, as the result of experience in the legislature at Albany, begun rather timidly to strive for social and industrial justice. But at that time my attitude was that of giving justice from above. It was the experience on the range that first taught me to try to get justice for all of us by working on the same level with the rest of my fellow citizens.

It was the conviction that there was much social and industrial injustice and the effort to secure social and industrial justice that first led me to taking so keen an interest in popular rule.

For years I accepted the theory, as most of the rest of us then accepted it, that we already had popular government; that this was a government by the people. I believed the power of the boss was due only to the indifference and short-sightedness of the average decent citizen. Gradually it came over me that while this was half the truth, it was only half the truth, and that while the boss owed part of his power to the fact that the average man did not do his duty, yet that there was the further fact to be considered, that for the average man it had already been made very difficult instead of very easy for him to do his duty. I grew to feel a keen interest in the machinery for getting adequate and genuine popular rule, chiefly because I found that we could not get social and industrial justice without popular rule, and that it was immensely easier to get such popular rule by the means of machinery of the type of direct nominations at primaries, the short ballot, the initiative, referendum, and the like.

I usually found that my interest in any given side of a question of justice was aroused by some concrete case. It was the examination I made into the miseries attendant upon the manufacture of cigars in tenement-houses that first opened my eyes to the need of legislation on such subjects. My friends come from many walks of life. The need for a workmen's compensation act was driven home to me by my knowing a brakeman who had lost his legs in an accident, and whose family was thereby at once reduced from self-respecting comfort to conditions that at one time became very dreadful. Of course, after coming across various concrete instances of this kind, I would begin to read up on the subject, and then I would get in touch with social workers and others who were experts and could acquaint me with what was vital in the matter. Looking back, it seems to me that I made my greatest strides forward while I was police commissioner, and this largely through my intimacy with Jacob Riis, for he opened all kinds of windows into the matter for me.

The conservation movement I approached from slightly different lines. I have always been fond of history and of science, and what has occurred to Spain, to Palestine, to China, and to North Africa from the destruction of natural resources is familiar to me. I have always been deeply impressed with Liebig's statement that it was the decrease of soil fertility, and not either peace or war, which was fundamental in bringing about the decadence of nations. While unquestionably nations have been destroyed by other causes, I have become convinced that it was the destruction of the soil itself which was perhaps the most fatal of all causes.

But when, at the beginning of my term of service as President, under the influence of Mr. Pinchot and Mr. Newell, I took up the cause of conservation, I was already fairly well awake to the need of social and industrial justice; and from the outset we had in view, not only the preservation of natural resources, but the prevention of monopoly in natural resources, so that they should inhere in the people as a whole. There were plenty of newspapers, the New York *Times, Sun,* and *Evening Post,* for instance, which cordially supported our policy of conservation as long as we did not try to combine it with a movement against monopolization of resources, and which promptly abandoned us when it became evident that we wished to conserve the resources not for a part of the people but for all of the people.

The country-life movement was simply another side of this movement for a better and juster life. From Mary E. Wilkins to Sarah O. Jewett, in story after story which I would read for mere enjoyment, I would come upon things that not merely pleased me but gave me instruction—I have always thought that a good novel or a good story could teach quite as much as a more solemnly pretentious work, if it was written in the right way and read in the right way— and then my experience on farms, my knowledge of farmers, the way I followed what happened to the sons and daughters of the farmers I knew, all joined to make me feel the need of arousing the public interest and the public conscience as regards the conditions of life in the country.

Here again I have been fortunate enough to live with my own people, and not to live as an outsider, but as a man doing his share of the work. I know what the work and what the loneliness of a farmer's life too often are. I do not want to help the farmer or to help his wife in ways that will soften either, but I do want to join with both, and try to help them and help myself and help all of us, not by doing away with the need of work, but by trying to create a situation in which work will be more fruitful, and in which the work shall produce and go hand in hand with opportunities for self-development.

Very early I learned through my reading of history, and I found through my association with reformers, that one of the prime difficulties was to get the man who wished reform within a nation also to pay heed to the needs of the nation from the international standpoint. Every little city or republic of antiquity was continually torn between factions which wished to do justice at home but were weak abroad, and other factions which secured justice abroad by the loss of personal liberty at home. So here at home I too often found that men who were ardent for social and industrial reform would be ignorant of the needs of this nation as a nation, would be ignorant of what the navy meant to the nation, of what it meant to the nation to have and to fortify and protect the Panama Canal, of what it meant to the nation to get from the other nations of mankind the respect which comes only to the just, and which is denied to the weaker nation far more quickly than it is denied to the stronger.

It ought not to be necessary to insist upon a point like this, with China before our very eyes offering the most woful example of the ruin that comes to a nation which cannot defend itself against aggression—and China, by the way, offers the further proof that centuries of complete absence of militarism may yet result in the development of all the worst vices and all the deepest misery that grow up in nations that suffer from overmuch militarism. Here again I learn from books, I learn from study, and I learn most by dealing with men.

I feel that the Progressive party owes no small part of its strength to the fact that it not only stands for the most far-reaching measures of social and industrial reform, but in sane and temperate fashion stands also for the right and duty of this nation to take a position of self-respecting strength among the nations of the world, to take such a position as will do injustice to no foreign power, strong or weak, and yet will show that it has both the spirit and the strength to repel injustice from abroad.

From *The Naval War of 1812:* Excerpts from the Summary to Chapter 9

In summing up the results of the struggle on the ocean it is to be noticed that very little was attempted, and nothing done, by the American Navy that could *materially* affect the result of the war. Commodore Rodgers' expedition after the Jamaica plate fleet failed; both the efforts to get a small squadron into the East Indian waters also miscarried; and otherwise the whole history of the struggle on the ocean is, as regards the Americans, only the record of individual cruises and fights. The material results were not very great, at least in their effect on Great Britain, whose enormous navy did not feel in the slightest degree the loss of a few frigates and sloops. But morally the result was of inestimable benefit to the United States. The victories kept up the spirits of the people, cast down by the defeats on land; practically decided in favor of the Americans the chief question in dispute—Great Britain's right of search and impressment—and gave the navy, and thereby the country, a world-wide reputation. I doubt if ever before a nation gained so much honor by a few single-ship duels. For there can be no question which side came out of the war with the greatest credit. The damage inflicted by each on the other was not very unequal in amount, but the balance was certainly in favor of the United States. . . .

But the comparative material loss gives no idea of the comparative honor gained. The British navy, numbering at the outset a thousand cruisers, had accomplished less than the American, which numbered but a dozen. Moreover, most of the loss suffered by the former was in single fight, while this had been but twice the case with the Americans, who had generally been overwhelmed by numbers. . . .

The Republic of the United States owed a great deal to the excellent make and armament of its ships, but it owed still more to the men who were in them. The massive timbers and heavy guns of *Old Ironsides* would have availed but little had it not been for her able commanders and crews. Of all the excellent single-ship captains, British or American, produced by the war, the palm should be awarded to Hull.[1] The deed of no other man (excepting Macdonough) equalled his escape from Broke's five ships, or surpassed his half-hour's conflict with the *Guerrière*. After him, almost all the American captains deserve high praise—Decatur, Jones, Blakely, Biddle, Bainbridge, Lawrence, Burrows, Allen, Warrington, Stewart, Porter. It is no small glory to a country to have had such men upholding the honor of its flag. On a par with the best of them are Broke, Manners, and also Byron and Blythe. It must be but a poor-spirited American whose veins do not tingle with pride when he reads of the cruises and fights of the sea-captains, and their grim prowess, which kept the old Yankee flag floating over the waters of the Atlantic for three years, in the teeth of the mightiest naval power the world has ever seen; but it is equally impossible not to admire Broke's chivalric challenge and successful fight, or the heroic death of the captain of the *Reindeer*.

Nor can the war ever be fairly understood by any one who does not bear in mind that the combatants were men of the same stock, who far more nearly resembled each other than either resembled any other nation. I honestly believe

---

[1]See "Naval Tactics," by Commander J. H. Ward, and "Life of Commodore Tatnall," by Charles C. Jones, Jr.

that the American sailor offered rather better material for a man-of-warsman than the British, because the freer institutions of his country (as compared with the Britain of the drunken Prince Regent and his dotard feather—a very different land from the present free England) and the peculiar exigencies of his life tended to make him more intelligent and self-reliant; but the difference, when there was any, was very small, and disappeared entirely when his opponents had been drilled for any length of time by men like Broke or Manners. The advantage consisted in the fact that our *average* commander was equal to the best, and higher than the average, of the opposing captains; and this held good throughout the various grades of the officers. The American officers knew they had redoubtable foes to contend with, and made every preparation accordingly. Owing their rank to their own exertions, trained by practical experience and with large liberty of action, they made every effort to have their crews in the most perfect state of skill and discipline. . . . The American prepared himself in every possible way; the Briton tried to cope with courage alone against courage united to skill. . . .

From *The Winning of the West*: Note to Chapter 4

It is greatly to be wished that some competent person would write a full and true history of our national dealings with the Indians. Undoubtedly the latter have often suffered terrible injustice at our hands. A number of instances, such as the conduct of the Georgians to the Cherokees in the early part of the present century, or the whole treatment of Chief Joseph and his Nez Percés, might be mentioned, which are indelible blots on our fair fame; and yet, in describing our dealings with the red men as a whole, historians do us much less than justice.

It was wholly impossible to avoid conflicts with the

weaker race, unless we were willing to see the American continent fall into the hands of some other strong power; and even had we adopted such a ludicrous policy, the Indians themselves would have made war upon us. It cannot be too often insisted that they did not own the land; or, at least, that their ownership was merely such as that claimed often by our own white hunters. If the Indians really owned Kentucky in 1775, then in 1776 it was the property of Boone and his associates; and to dispossess one party was as great a wrong as to dispossess the other. To recognize the Indian ownership of the limitless prairies and forests of this continent—that is, to consider the dozen squalid savages who hunted at long intervals over a territory of a thousand square miles as owning it outright—necessarily implies a similar recognition of the claims of every white hunter, squatter, horse thief, or wandering cattleman. Take as an example the country round the Little Missouri. When the cattlemen, the first actual settlers, came into this land in 1882, it was already scantily peopled by a few white hunters and trappers. The latter were extremely jealous of intrusion; they had held their own in spite of the Indians, and, like the Indians, the inrush of settlers and the consequent destruction of the game meant their own undoing; also, again like the Indians, they felt that their having hunted over the soil gave them a vague prescriptive right to its sole occupation, and they did their best to keep actual settlers out. In some cases, to avoid difficulty, their nominal claims were bought up; generally, and rightly, they were disregarded. Yet they certainly had as good a right to the Little Missouri country as the Sioux have to most of the land on their present reservations. In fact, the mere statement of the case is sufficient to show the absurdity of asserting that the land really belonged to the Indians. The different tribes have always been utterly unable to define their own boundaries. Thus the Delawares and Wyandots, in 1785, though entirely separate nations, claimed and, in a certain sense, occupied almost exactly the same territory.

Moreover, it was wholly impossible for our policy to be always consistent. Nowadays we undoubtedly ought to break up the great Indian reservations, disregard the tribal governments, allot the land in severalty (with, however, only a limited power of alienation), and treat the Indians as we do other citizens, with certain exceptions, for their sakes as well as ours. But this policy, which it would be wise to follow now, would have been wholly impracticable a century since. Our central government was then too weak either effectively to control its own members or adequately to punish aggressions made upon them; and even if it had been strong, it would probably have proved impossible to keep entire order over such a vast, sparsely peopled frontier, with such turbulent elements on both sides. The Indians could not be treated as individuals at that time. There was no possible alternative, therefore, to treating their tribes as nations, exactly as the French and English had done before us. Our difficulties were partly inherited from these, our predecessors, were partly caused by our own misdeeds, but were mainly the inevitable result of the conditions under which the problem had to be solved; no human wisdom or virtue could have worked out a peaceable solution. As a nation, our Indian policy is to be blamed, because of the weakness it displayed, because of its shortsightedness, and its occasional leaning to the policy of the sentimental humanitarians; and we have often promised what was impossible to perform; but there has been little wilful wrong-doing. Our government almost always tried to act fairly by the tribes; the governmental agents (some of whom have been dishonest, and others foolish, but who, as a class, have been greatly traduced), in their reports, are far more apt to be unjust to the whites than to the reds; and the federal authorities, though unable to prevent much of the injustice, still did check and control the white borderers very much more effectually than the Indian sachems and war-chiefs controlled their young braves. The tribes were warlike and bloodthirsty, jealous of each other and of the whites; they claimed the land for their hunting-grounds, but their claims all conflicted with one another; their knowledge of their own boundaries was so indefinite that they were always willing, for inadequate compensation, to sell land to which they had merely the vaguest title; and yet, when once they had received the goods, were generally reluctant to make over even what they could; they coveted the goods and scalps of the whites, and the young warriors were always on the alert to commit outrages when they could do it with impunity. On the other hand, the evil-disposed whites regarded the Indians as fair game for robbery and violence of any kind; and the far larger number of well-disposed men, who would not willingly wrong any Indian, were themselves maddened by the memories of hideous injuries received. They bitterly resented the action of the government, which, in their eyes, failed to properly protect them and yet sought to keep them out of waste, uncultivated lands which they did not regard as being any more the property of the Indians than of their own hunters. With the best intentions, it was wholly impossible for any government to evolve order out of such a chaos without resort to the ultimate arbitrator—the sword.

The purely sentimental historians take no account of the difficulties under which we labored nor of the countless wrongs and provocations we endured, while grossly magnifying the already lamentably large number of injuries for which we really deserve to be held responsible. To get a fair idea of the Indians of the present day, and of our dealings with them, we have fortunately one or two excellent books, notably "Hunting Grounds of the Great West" and "Our Wild Indians," by Colonel Richard I. Dodge (Hartford, 1882); and "Massacres of the Mountains," by J. P. Dunn (New York, 1886). As types of the opposite class, which are worse than valueless, and which nevertheless might cause some hasty future historian, unacquainted with the facts, to fall into grievous error, I may mention "A Century of Dishonor," by H. H. (Mrs. Helen Hunt Jackson), and "Our Indian Wards" (George W. Manypenny). The latter is a mere spiteful diatribe against various army officers, and neither its manner nor its matter warrants more than an allusion. Mrs. Jackson's book is capable of doing more harm because it is written in good English, and because the author, who had lived a pure and noble life, was intensely in earnest in what she wrote, and had the most praiseworthy purpose—to prevent our committing any more injustice to the Indians. This was all most proper; every good man or woman should do whatever is possible to make the government treat the Indians of the present time in the fairest and most generous spirit, and to provide against any repetition of such outrages as were inflicted upon the Nez Percés and upon part of the Cheyennes, or the wrongs with which the civilized nations of the Indian Territory are sometimes threatened. The purpose of the book is excellent, but the spirit in which it is written cannot be called even technically honest. As a polemic, it is possible that it did not do harm (though the effect of even a polemic is marred by hysterical indifference to facts). As a history it would be beneath criticism, were it not that the high character of the author and her excellent literary work in other directions have given it a fictitious value and made it much quoted by the large class of amiable but maudlin fanatics concerning whom it may be said that the excellence of their intentions but indifferently atones for the invariable folly and ill effect of their actions. It is not too much to say that the book is thoroughly untrustworthy from cover to cover, and that not a single statement it contains should be accepted without independent proof; for even those that are not absolutely false are often as bad on account of so much of the truth having been suppressed. One effect of this is, of course, that the author's recitals of the many real wrongs of Indian tribes utterly fail to impress us, because she lays quite as much stress on those that are nonexistent, and on the equally numerous cases where the wrongdoing was wholly the other way. To get an idea of the value of the work, it is only necessary to compare her statements about almost any tribe with the real facts, choosing at random; for instance, compare her accounts of the Sioux and the plains tribes generally with those given by Colonel Dodge in his two books; or her recital of the Sandy Creek massacre with the facts as stated by Mr. Dunn—who is apt, if anything, to lean to the Indian's side.

These foolish sentimentalists not only write foul slanders about their own countrymen, but are themselves the worst possible advisers on any point touching Indian management. They would do well to heed General Sheridan's bitter words, written when many Easterners were clamoring against the army authorities because they took partial vengeance for a series of brutal outrages: "I do not know how far these humanitarians should be excused on account of their ignorance; but surely it is the only excuse that can give a shadow of justification for aiding and abetting such horrid crimes."